WHERE'S MY
MATE?

WHERE'S MY
MATE?

BETHANY K. SCANLON

TATE PUBLISHING *& Enterprises*

Published by Tate Publishing & Enterprises, LLC
127 E. Trade Center Terrace | Mustang, Oklahoma 73064 USA
1.888.361.9473 | www.tatepublishing.com

Tate Publishing is committed to excellence in the publishing industry. The company reflects the philosophy established by the founders, based on Psalms 68:11,
"The Lord gave the word and great was the company of those who published it."

Book design copyright © 2007 by Tate Publishing, LLC. All rights reserved.
Cover design by Janae J. Glass
Interior design by Jacob Crisusp

Published in the United States of America

ISBN: 978-1-60247-545-8
1. Christian Living: Relationships   2. Dating, Loving, & Marriage
09.18.20

ACKNOWLEDGMENTS

I give God Almighty my eternal gratitude for loving me and accepting me just the way I am and giving me the grace to write this book.

I want to thank my wonderful and patient husband Luke for loving me like Christ loves His church. I love you, Luke!

Thank you, Chris and Stacey Loeffler, for your love, support, prayers, and help. Thank you for believing in me and the success of this book.

Thank you, Jeremy and Stephanie Hendrix, for your trust. May goodness and mercy follow you all the days of your life.

To my friend Christine Dickson: thank you for believing God with me to move mountains and touch other people's lives.

Special thanks to all of my bridesmaids (Christine,

Holly, Jennie, Susan and Erin) who walked with me and supported me during a trying time.

INTRODUCTION

I know firsthand the frustration of having a desire to be married and wondering where my mate was. I am a romantic at heart and love stories are always a favorite with me. I have watched so many single men and women of God walking around with the desire to be married but not knowing exactly what to do about it. That is what this book is about, how to get from wanting to be married to being married.

It is my desire to see God's children prosper and do what He has called them to do. I believe that it is God's will that the majority of single Christians are happily married. When the Lord first led me to write this book, I was nervous because of the content of my testimony. However, my will is submitted to His and I know that He wants to bless many people with this book, so as you read it may God reveal His purpose for your life concerning marriage.

TABLE OF CONTENTS

WILD HORSES COULDN'T DRAG
ME AWAY!

On April 3, 1998, my husband Ben came home with one of his drinking buddies, told me he had filed for divorce and was moving out. Then, as he was in the bedroom packing his bags, his friend grabbed me inappropriately and said something to the tune of "Now that you're single..." It felt like someone had stabbed me in the heart and then twisted the knife! How did I get here with my life? Where did I go so wrong? I guess we should start from the beginning...

When I was in seventh grade, I was planning to commit suicide one night and had purposed in my heart to do it the next morning. Before I went to bed, I got down on one knee and prayed, "If there is a God, this is the time to show Yourself to me." The very next morning, my mom walked into my room and said she was sending me to my biological dad's house located in a suburb of Chicago. (My parents divorced when I was two, and my mom remarried when I was three.) I knew this was an answer to my prayer. When I went to school in Chicago, I met a nice girl named Kelly from Japan who was a Buddhist. Kelly was one of the only girls who was kind to me at my new school, while the rest of the kids made fun of my Texas drawl. I practiced Buddhism with her in search of this God who had answered my prayer. I even went with her to a Buddhist temple to be dedicated to Buddha. I prayed religiously, went to functions and did everything that I was told to do with Kelly's parents helping me every step of the way. I went to this extreme partly because I was always a curious child, but mostly because I very much needed stability, and I desperately wanted to be loved. The devastation of my childhood was almost too much to bear at times, and I was looking for any glimmer of hope for a better life. Much to my disappointment, I still had no inner peace or healing so I eventually gave up Buddhism. Also during these years, my step-mom was a Mason, so I was able to join and become a Rainbow girl. I performed all of the ceremonies at the Masonic Temple that I was supposed to, but I never found any spiritual satisfaction in that crowd either so I quit a few years later.

Toward the end of this season, my biological dad stole some jewelry from his mother-in-law and had it blamed on me. It was horrible; the police harassed me about giving back the jewelry and they questioned my school friends and their parents. The only family that believed that I had not done it was Kelly's family while my other friends' parents forbid them to associate with me. My stepfamily thought that I was the thief, and they wanted nothing to do with me. Crushed, I moved back to Houston. Not long afterwards, my step-mom finally got fed up with my dad's antics and they divorced.

Some time passed, and things got worse. Back in Houston, and a junior in high school, my step-dad asked me to leave home (I was sixteen) after I was caught skipping school and smoking. I was a very distraught teenager and happy to leave home because of the verbal and physical abuse that I suffered there on almost a daily basis since I was four or five years old. My mom used to tell me often how much she hated me and wished that she aborted me. She would also call me stupid and tell me that I was a "commoner" who would never amount to anything. She used to threaten to dump me off somewhere and drive off. She would say that the only thing I would ever be good at was cleaning the house. When I was nine years old, I attended a private school and on picture day when it was mandatory that I wore a skirt, the teacher saw all of my welts and bruises. The principal called my parents for an explanation. When I got home from the ordeal, my mom put me on a guilt trip and told me that I was such a bad kid that I deserved the beatings. About a month later my parents pulled me out of the school. My step-dad used to spank me with a 2x4 while my mom held me down, and I would have bruises so bad on my rear end that I could not sit for days. Sometimes he used his fists, other times his belt. He also used to call me Cinderella and force me to clean the house constantly. As you can imagine, my grades in school were terrible (except for English and drama), and I acted out quite a bit.

When I left home, I figured that anywhere I went was better than what was going on there. After I started living on my own, I got drunk almost every night, did drugs, and smoked about two packs of cigarettes a day. Still searching, I visited palm readers, mediums, and studied my astrological sign, but I never found any real answers to life's questions. My depression increased, as did my drug and alcohol intake. After about a year of being on my own, my biological dad asked me if I would move to the panhandle of Florida with him. I did and went to high school in Ft. Walton Beach for my senior year. I constantly worked after school at night to have enough money to pay for rent and other bills since my dad didn't get a job when we arrived and he hadn't changed from when I was a teenager. I did find some light however; that year I made a friend named Jessie. Her relationship would mean more to me than I could know. We became roommates after I graduated, and, following meeting some cute guys from New Orleans and having fun during Mardi Gras, we decided that New Orleans was our destiny.

While Jessie and I were driving around New Orleans (a couple of hours after we had signed a year-long lease on an apartment) a drunk driver hit us hard on the passenger side of our small blue Volkswagen Cabriolet.

We were not wearing seatbelts, and I was sitting in the passenger's seat. I felt myself lift completely off the seat, and my head was about to go through the windshield when I felt two huge hands on my shoulders. Those hands pushed me back in my seat and held me in place till the car stopped moving. At the same time, Jessie felt a huge hand on her chest hold her down and absorb the impact. As they towed away a completely totaled car, the officer remarked that he could not believe we were not hurt. I knew after the accident that there was definitely a spirit world and that there just might be angels. Only something good could have protected us.

When Jessie and I shared what happened to each other, Jessie was convinced that the only reason we were okay was because her Christian parents were praying for us. That was my first experience with the power of God's angels. It turned out that I would have more encounters with angels later on.

Weeks later, crying and depressed because my boyfriend would not commit (I wanted to marry him), I told Jessie I felt I couldn't go on. She looked at me and said, "You've tried everything else, why don't you try God?" Mind you, she was a backslidden Christian, but she still believed the Bible was true and that God, Satan, angels, and demons did exist. When she said that, I thought, *Well, why not?* I ran to my room and pulled out a small Gideon Bible I had been given by a couple when I waited tables for a few weeks. I was too superstitious to throw it away. Inside the back cover was the salvation prayer; I prayed it, and as soon as

I did I felt every last bit of the depression leave and something refreshing come inside of me. I knew the Bible was true and Jesus was alive. I got down on my knees and asked God to send me a husband and if my boyfriend was not the one, would He please move him out of my life.

About a week later, my boyfriend informed me that his company wanted him to transfer immediately out of state and travel around the world on business. He told me he could not see me anymore. After that I knew God had answered my prayer, and I began going to church and I was water baptized. However, I chose to keep living the party lifestyle. My next big encounter with God happened a little later. During a routine gynecologist check-up, the doctors discovered abnormal cell growth. A biopsy revealed cancer, and I was devastated by the diagnosis. After seeing two doctors, they finally scheduled me for surgery to try to remove the cancer, but I was told it might be too late, that it might have started to spread to my female organs. The fear and inner turmoil I went through was almost unbearable, but my roommate Jessie told me that people sometimes got healed supernaturally through the power of God. I prayed again.

The night before the surgery, I got up the nerve to visit a church outside New Orleans in Harvey called White Dove Fellowship. I had been watching the services on TV at about four in the morning after I got off work. I went with a guy friend, and we sat in the very back, trying to stay unnoticed. While the pastor was preaching, I felt something like a cloud come over me, and I felt very sleepy. I heard an audible voice speak in my left ear and it said, "You've already met your soul mate, you'll be with him soon." It repeated that about three times. At the same time I saw a picture of big beautiful green eyes come into focus before me. The voice sounded so beautiful I was sure it was an angel. I whispered back to the voice and started naming off the different guys I was currently dating and asked if one of them was my soul mate. The voice responded "no" to every name I mentioned. When the cloud lifted, it was like I had awoken from a dream, and I was able to watch the rest of the service. When the sermon was over, another minister walked up to the stage and said, "There is a man in here, and you are on drugs. God is healing you now. There is also a lady here who is supposed to go to surgery tomorrow to take care of a disease in her female parts; God is healing you now."

As soon as he said that I felt this power shoot through me, and I just *knew* I was healed. Several different doctors confirmed this later. My friend looked at me and said, "God just healed me—I was the one on drugs. I felt my mind clear up when that man spoke those words." He also told me he heard the voice telling me I was going to meet my soul mate soon. By the way, in case you are wondering, I was completely sober because of anticipating surgery the next morning. Several months later, Jessie got pregnant and moved home to Destin, Florida, with her parents to help raise the baby.

Shortly thereafter a man named Ben with big green eyes who Jessie and I already knew from his visits to the club I worked at, took me out partying one night. One thing led to another, and we eventually fell in love and moved in together. During this time Jessie started attending revival meetings in Pensacola, Florida, at Brownsville Assembly of God. She would call me in New Orleans and tell me I was going to go to hell if I did not get out of sin and get in a right relationship with God. One time, Ben and I went to Florida to visit Jessie and my dad, and while I was there, Jessie convinced me to attend a revival service with her, and I did, but I refused to repent. While Jessie and I were at church that night, my dad took Ben to Hooters and then to a strip club, got him drunk and tried to set him up with another woman. Discouraged, I just wanted to go back home to New Orleans. Ben and I married shortly after that visit, and the day we got married, I called Jessie and informed her that I was not in sin anymore.

Six months later, after a long nasty Halloween night in the French Quarter with Ben and some co-workers, I had to put Ben in jail for domestic violence. I didn't know what to do, so I called Jessie in desperation for a place to visit while I cleared my head. She told me I could visit her if, and only if, I agreed to attend church with her. I agreed, because after the police left my house, I asked God what to do, and I heard the song "Mercy Seat" in my spirit. I had heard the song once before when I had visited the revival meeting with her. So off to Florida I went, and back to a revival meeting. This time I listened. The preacher, Steve Hill, said something to the effect that if your life isn't going right "it is because the wages of sin is death." A light bulb went off! I knew why my life was a series of one bad event after another and why I never had inner peace. I had been in sin, doing wrong things, and I had to change. Then, of all things, a lady got up and started singing "Mercy Seat." I ran, no flew, to the altar and completely surrendered my life to Christ and repented of my sin.

I went back to the revival the next night, and that weekend I visited Jessie's church in Destin where they were having a women's meeting. At the end, they said if anyone needed prayer, to go up to a prayer warrior. I walked up to a nice-looking man and woman and said, "I have been drinking, smoking, and doing drugs, and I don't want to do it anymore." They laid hands on me and prayed in tongues, telling demons to leave. I stood there, my eyes closed tight till they were finished, said thank you, and left. I felt great! I had been smoking two packs of cigarettes a day and after they prayed I had no desire to smoke cigarettes or do drugs. I was completely free!

I talked to my husband after he got out of jail, and we agreed to try to make a go of it. He came to pick me up that Monday, and the first thing he did was kindly offer me a cigarette and I told him I had quit. After that he tried to take me to a bar to get drunk, and I told him I had quit that too. He was nice and supportive at first, hoping I would grow out of my religious phase, but when I continued to refuse the party lifestyle, he said I wasn't really his wife because I was not the same person he had married. His dad was also telling him our marriage wasn't valid because the ceremony was not performed in the Catholic Church. Ben grew resentful and started going out with his friends, and I would not hear from him for days at a time. One night when he was home, he arose from our bed and walked over to my Bible and urinated on it. He had absolutely no recollection he had committed this act the next day. I had to show him my Bible and the puddle to prove it. One day he sat next to me on the couch and very calmly asked me to pick between Jesus or him. I told him "Jesus." Shortly thereafter he filed for divorce. During the divorce, a lady with a prophetic gift prayed with me and told me that the voice that spoke in my ear about my "soul mate" at church was *not* God but a demon appearing as an angel of light, and that Satan had set me up with this man in an attempt to destroy me. The reason I had fallen for it was because I had refused to stay out of sin and study God's Word. Honestly, I did not like this woman at all, and I figured she was wrong because I thought, *How could a loving God let this happen to me?* Later, of course, I realized she was correct and I repented. The divorce was intense, and I felt very alone. I was so hurt that I would just watch TV when I wasn't at church or work and eat all of the foods that I normally didn't and gained about forty pounds. Since we worked together at the same office and we were divorcing (I left the club a few months after we were married), I had to quit so I took a job working at a hotel on Canal Street. He also had me thrown out of our home, so I rented someone's pool house to live in and took the city bus to work and church.

I immersed myself in the Word of God and was at church every time the doors opened. After some time passed and I learned more about who God was, I decided to pray specifically for what characteristics I wanted in a mate. I wrote out a list and asked the Lord to send me someone who was a match to that list. I prayed and prayed asking God to send me a husband. A few months later, I received a prophecy stating that God was going to send me a husband soon and that he was going to be a man of God who was going to walk beside me. Since the prophecy said soon, I thought that meant the next day. I was on the lookout. Lo and behold, a couple of days later a guy named Darin, who looked like James Dean, was hired at my work. When I first laid eyes on him, a strong thought shot through my mind: *This is your new husband.* I was so excited!

It turned out that Darin was a gambler who got drunk almost every night and was addicted to pornography, but I thought, *Hey, I can fix that! God wants me to lead him to Jesus and then he will be a great husband and match my list! I know this is of God!* So I dragged him to church, informed him we would not be having sex till we were married, and made him pray and attend church with me. However, he never stopped gambling or using pornography—or anything else for that matter.

I was very discouraged. At church one of the ladies came up to me after service and said, "Do you think he is supposed to be your husband?"

I sheepishly said, "Maybe."

She responded, "He isn't ready yet." She also graciously invited me to her home later that day. When I arrived she politely asked if she could pray for me. I agreed, and after she prayed I heard the Lord's still small voice speak to me clearly. "The reason you are trying so hard with Darin is because you feel like you failed with Ben." All of a sudden I felt completely free because I had my answer! However, my romantic feelings for this man were still there. Later, when Darin and I were sitting on my couch giving each other gaga eyes, I felt something slide over my heart and I heard a clicking sound as if a lock was turning. I knew it was the Holy Spirit and all of a sudden I had no more feelings for Darin, I only loved him like a brother. I broke off the relationship and returned to the single life. By the way, after that relationship, I added a lot more to my list!

Shortly after that, the Lord prompted me to move back to Houston and move in with my parents. While there, I tried going on several different dates with men I had met on an Internet dating service. They claimed to be Christian; I say claimed because the Bible states that if you are a hearer of the Word and not a doer, you are deceiving yourself. Almost every man I went on a date with was not a doer of the Word and did not think twice about cussing, drinking, and having sex outside of wedlock. None of these dates lasted past one or two. I did end up leading two of my "Christian" dates to the Lord and into a real relationship with Christ. Several months later, I moved from my parents' house to a one-bedroom apartment while working at a retail clothing store and attending Lakewood Church.

In prayer one afternoon, I felt strongly impressed in my spirit that the Lord was about to move me to a smaller church. One day when I was visiting my mother, she said, "You have an apartment, a job, and a car; all you need now is a boyfriend. Why don't you get on the computer again and find yourself a man?" I argued with her a little bit, telling her I had already tried that and nothing happened. To get her off my back, I got on the computer and pulled up a personal ad called "Are you a Proverbs 31 woman?" The man in the picture was very good looking, and he stated he was looking for a wife who was committed to the Lord Jesus Christ. I thought, *This guy is perfect to write to because it will get my mother to leave me alone.* My mom did not like my becoming a Christian because she was an atheist and most certainly did not approve of me marrying another Christian. She looked at the personal ad and said, "What is it you like about this guy?" I told her it was because he was a Christian. When I told her my motivation for looking at his profile, she said I could no longer use her computer to look up personals if I was going to insist on dating Christians. I told her okay, but I had already sent this man a quick email, telling him I would like to talk to him on the phone. I left her house not thinking twice about that email.

Interestingly enough, a few days prior, I had been feeling unusually frustrated because I had been praying for a mate for about two years and there seemed to be no one in sight. I cried out before the Lord in desperation, reminding Him that His Word in Isaiah says, "None shall lack for her mate," and I was *definitely* lacking. During that prayer, I sensed the Lord's presence very strongly and felt something like a ring slide over my left ring finger. I felt a burden lift off me and supernatural peace fill me. I knew everything was going to be okay and that God would work it out. That was early May 2000. While I was at work I kept sensing a lot of joy and I remembered the email I had sent to the Christian man. Finally, after a couple of days, I went back to my mom's house and checked email. The Christian had written back! We talked on the phone for about a week, and I was so excited! I prayed and asked the Lord if he was "the one," and I heard the still small voice tell me, "He is the forerunner to your mate."

The Christian invited me to a singles Bible study he was teaching, so I dressed up in my best outfit and went. When I arrived, he was in the kitchen talking to someone. When he found out I was there, he didn't even bother to walk over and say hello. I positioned myself on the couch on the farthest end by the door so I could run out at any given time. I felt very rejected, since this guy had never seen me before and now that he saw what I looked like, he didn't want to say "Hi."

I was very insecure; since I was a teenager, I struggled with my weight. At that time I was about thirty pounds overweight and very embarrassed about it. After the lesson started, I noticed one of the men staring at me. I thought to myself, *You wish, buddy!* He was definitely not my type, plus he was bragging about playing the drums, and musicians were never the kind of guys I dated.

Finally, the Christian said hello to me and walked me out to my car, and drummer boy followed. I thought, *Oh great, I wish he would just go away!* I got in my car and left, thinking I was never going to see those people again. However, I kept feeling impressed by the Lord to visit their church on Sunday. I went, and the Christian sat by me but made it pretty obvious he just wanted to be friends. I went back Tuesday to some special teaching service they were having. One of the girls, Holly, whom I had met at the Bible study, asked if I would attend the church's Tuesday night prayer meeting. When she asked, I sensed joy in my spirit like I was supposed to go, so I did.

When I showed up at the prayer meeting, I looked for the Christian but he was not there. Instead, drummer boy was there and was leading the meeting. As the prayer meeting concluded, I was walking out when I accidentally dropped my keys. Drummer boy handed them back and told me he sensed I had "trust issues." I thought, *This man is a complete nut, and I need to nip this in the bud so he knows to leave me alone.* So I replied very sarcastically, "Why don't you pray for me then?"

By that time two other people had joined us, and we all prayed for my trust issues. While they were praying, the Lord spoke to me in what sounded like an audible voice inside of me and told me I was going to be his (drummer boy's) wife. *What!* I couldn't believe it! *Him?* After they said, "Amen," I took off out of there and had a very serious talk with God. I asked Him if He was sure He had the right person.

The following night I visited Grace Community Church in Clear Lake to listen to Steve Hill preach. Visiting from Florida, he was the preacher who taught on sin when I committed my life to Christ and that night he was preaching on receiving a crown after you die. I remember wondering what type of crown I was going to receive when my time came. After the sermon I walked to the front to receive prayer from one of the ministers. When my turn came, the minister asked what I wanted prayer for and I told him I didn't know. He pointed his finger at me without touching me and said, "You're about to be married." The power of God hit me when he said that and I fell back, right on my rear end while drummer boy's face flashed before my eyes. I later found out his name was Luke. I didn't know what to expect! Was Luke going to come up to me and ask me to marry him? I wasn't going to approach him!

I continued to attend the small church where God had sent me, but Luke did not give me the time of day and I ignored him. I attended the prayer meeting the following Tuesday, and Luke prophesied over everyone at the meeting including me. He told me again I had trust issues and that he saw a crown of beauty on my head. The next night, the singles met together to watch a movie at someone's house. After the movie when Luke and some others were in the kitchen, I asked Luke what a crown of beauty was since I had never heard of it. I still thought he was a little flaky, since I just knew there was no way *I* could ever have *any* trust issues. One of the ladies whipped around and said, "That crown is from the scripture in Isaiah 62 where it says your land will never again be called forsaken or desolate; your new name is married!" When she said the word *married,* the power of God hit me and I crumpled to the kitchen floor. Embarrassingly enough, it was Luke and his roommate who helped me off the floor.

Weeks went by and Luke never made a move toward me and did not show any interest. I thought I had not heard from God and that maybe it was Satan tricking me again. After a night in heavy prayer, I woke up speaking in tongues and I received the interpretation immediately to what I had prayed. Part of the interpretation was that I was going to have a prophetic marriage and that God was going to speak to me more about my mate on June 19. I wrote down the entire prophecy, which also included something I was going to do in ministry, and then I forgot about it.

While all this drama was going on in my personal life, my work was also proving to be interesting. I had led my boss Christine, Christine's boss, and three other employees to Christ, and I was working hard to disciple them and bring them to church. During a lunch break, I was at a bookstore around the corner from work looking for a book by Elisabeth Elliot called *Passion and Purity*. I wanted to give it to one of the young single ladies I had led to Christ named Jennie. While looking for *Passion and Purity*, the Lord led me to buy the sequel as well, so I located the book and began to thumb through it. While I was reading and eating a grape Pop-Tart, the Holy Spirit touched me and I sensed the name "Lucas Scanlon" drop into my heart. I wrote down the date this happened, and wouldn't you know it, the date was June 19! When I finished lunch and came back out to the sales floor, Jennie and Christine said that my face was white as a ghost and they begged me to tell them what happened. I relented and told them about Luke and made them promise to keep it secret! I was again encouraged that I had heard from the Lord.

Later, I was at another singles Bible study and Luke was teaching. When he stood up to speak the opening scripture, it was Joshua 1:3 (that I had just been praying for Luke the night before!). When he spoke out the scripture, a huge angel appeared before me and threw what appeared to be fire into my belly and said, "Where Luke goes, you will go with him." When the "fire" hit me, it knocked me off my feet. Everyone got real quiet and looked at me funny. Luke asked after the Bible study what had happened, and I just shrugged my shoulders and blew it off—I wasn't going to tell anyone what had happened, especially him!

Later, a group of women from the church brought

me into a room during one of the Tuesday night prayer meetings and accused me of being demon possessed because they would see a physical reaction from the power of God working in my life. They told me that God would never work this way and that demons were taking over my body or that I was doing this for attention. They told me that our pastor had them all fasting and praying so I would get delivered from all these demons. The things they said hurt terribly and I felt betrayed by my own pastor. I went home and cried out to God, asking Him if it was the devil doing all this because I was still struggling with a fear of deception, having been previously deceived with Ben and Darin. The Lord asked me if I was serving men or Him. I told the Lord He could knock me to the ground as much as He liked in front of whomever He wanted to. The Lord also reminded me of a dream He had given me earlier. In the dream I saw the Holy Spirit trying to get Luke and I together and Satan standing between us. I also saw Holly in front of me with a big shield of faith, trying to guard me. Holly, by the way, did end up playing a big role by encouraging me and praying for me, and she was one of my bridesmaids.

A few more weeks passed, and Luke barely acknowledged my existence and I made sure to stay away from him. Also, during this time I became good friends with Holly, and one day when we were praying together, she looked at me and said, "The Lord just told me that you are going to marry Luke." I freaked out on her and told her she was wrong. I was afraid for anyone to find out

what had been happening to me. I had not told anyone except for Jennie and Christine for fear they would
think I was crazy. Another time I was praying with a
different friend from church, Erin, and in the middle
of prayer she told me God just told her that Luke was
my mate. I told her she must have missed God. After
some time, I finally confessed what was going on to my
girlfriends and made them promise not to say a word
to anyone, especially Luke. All were a huge comfort to
me, and they all ended up being my bridesmaids.

One day I was at a singles meeting and Luke sang
a solo, "Let the Peace of God Reign." When he sang
I heard a click that sounded like the unlocking of my
heart and I felt something slide off my heart, and all
of a sudden I was head over heels in love with Luke! It
scared me so badly I left the meeting.

I continued to try to avoid Luke; I don't know why,
except that I was afraid of rejection and he was not pay-
ing any attention to me. Again I was discouraged and
I prayed. The Lord woke me up at around two in the
morning one day, and I went to my living room and
prayed in the Spirit and listened to a sermon on tape.
All of a sudden I heard the Lord's voice as clear as a bell
in my spirit say, "Lucas is your mate." I sensed peace
wash over me. More weeks passed, and still nothing.

It was now September and I attended a meeting at
church where there was a prophet visiting. My current
boss and new friend, Christine, and I came into an
agreement prayer based on Matthew 18:19–20, and we
asked that the Lord would speak through the prophet

to us and confirm to me if Luke was my mate. He called up my friend to the front and I followed her. He prophesied over her and then turned to me. One of the things he said was, "You are facing a major decision right now, stand still and see the salvation of your Lord." I started crying. I knew the major decision was marriage and that I was on the right path. About two years earlier, the Lord had given me a Scripture promise for my mate from 2 Chronicles 2:17: "Stand still and see the salvation of your Lord."

A little while after that, I felt the Lord was leading me to a second job at a finance company. I took this job and wouldn't you know, after I was there, Luke was hired on. I was floored and a little scared. To make a long story short, my new boss at the finance company told me he was partnering me with Luke so Luke could train me. I knew what God was up to. So Luke started helping me study to pass a test I needed for work. We became friends: some days he would flirt, other days he was cold. I was really confused. I realized, as we became good friends, he was a match to my mate list.

One day at a singles meeting I asked for prayer, and they gathered around and prayed for me. I prayed (where no one could hear me) and asked God for a confirmation (again!) that Luke was my mate. Shortly thereafter, one of the guys in prayer looked at me and told me he believed God was telling him to communicate one word to me. When he spoke the word "destiny," the power of God hit me and again I was on the ground.

One day at work, Luke told me that he believed God had spoken to him about another woman and that she was his wife. When he said this, I felt supernatural peace wash over me. That still did not stop the tears; I cried for days and asked God how He could let something so cruel happen to me and that I was not going to be someone's second choice! I do not think I had ever been so upset in my entire life. The nerve! He was flirting with me, asking me to dinner and sometimes the movies, and then he tells me about some other girl! I called my boss and now friend Christine and asked her to pray with me. We prayed that if Luke was the one God truly ordained for me to marry, He would intervene immediately.

The next day at work, a man from church called me and said God had told him and his wife to hire me. I prayed about it because I knew Luke worked at this company, and I heard the still small voice tell me to walk by faith not by sight. I had already turned in my two weeks' notice at my job, and I could not seem to find another, so I took the job by faith. It turned out that Luke not only worked for this man but was told to train me so we had to ride around in the car for about four hours a day; plus, we had to do the second job together. I have to say I was pretty mean to him for a while because I was so hurt about him saying he was going to marry someone else.

Again, he would flirt with me and then turn cold. This made me furious! Somewhere during this time while I was working with Luke, I visited someone's house for a Bible study. This person did not attend my church, and I received a word from the Lord through a man who barely knew who I was. Basically, the word was that "Satan desired to sift me like wheat, but God was going to see me through." At a singles meeting one night, sometime during this entire mess, I also received a prophecy by someone that "God was about to part the Red Sea for me and I would soon see the other side."

Of course these people had no idea what they were saying, but I knew through these prophecies that God was trying to comfort me about Luke being so hot and cold with me. Another thing that happened is that I met a lady Christian at someone's house (who did not attend my church) and I confided in her everything that was happening. She recommended that we pray and ask the Lord to confirm His word to me through two or three witnesses. A few days later I visited a very small church I had never been to before. After worship, the pastor walked up to me and said, "I have a word from God for you, would you like to hear it?" I looked dumbfounded and nodded yes. The pastor said, "You are going to get it!" Then another man walked up and said, "God told me He has told you who your husband is and he is a true man of God and don't let anyone tell you any different."

I assure you, after that church service, all confusion, hurt, and pain left and wild horses couldn't drag me away from the fact that I knew Luke Scanlon was God's will for me concerning a mate. The next night, I was with Luke praying for his roommate, and he turned and looked and me and said, "God says that you are right!"

I said, "Right about what?"

He just smiled and said, "Marriage." When he said marriage, the power of God hit me, and I landed on my backside once again. That was the third witness.

On a side note, I am not sure why I am so sensitive to the power of God. When I first got saved, for several months I would watch preachers lay hands on people and the people would fall down. They would later talk about how God told them this and that. When they would lay hands on me, I would feel nothing and hear nothing. So I prayed for months that I would feel God's power and hear His voice, but I refused to just fall down. I wanted to know it was the Holy Spirit and not just my imagination. Also, on my mate list I wrote that I wanted to "know that I know beyond a shadow of a doubt who God had called me to marry." I believe a lot of what happened to me spiritually during this time in my life was an answer to those prayers.

For the next week, I teased Luke about the marriage prophecy he gave me to see if he would say anything. He never did and would continue to be cold to me. One day, his car broke down so I went to his house to give him a ride. When I got there he was very frosty to me and told me he had changed his mind about need-ing a ride and that he was going to fix his car. I got back in my car, cried, and then I prayed and asked for the Lord's intervention. When he drove off, his car stalled, and he called me and asked for a ride! We went to Bible study together and when I stopped to drop him off, we prayed together. There were a lot of weird problems going on with both our jobs, so when we prayed, I asked God if there was any disobedience in our lives. When I prayed, the Holy Spirit spoke the word *marriage* to my spirit, and I knew He spoke that to Luke also. Luke looked at me and said, "So what did He say to you?" I just smiled and shook my head "no," meaning I wasn't going to tell him. He looked at me and then asked me to marry him! The date was April 3, 2001. Of course, I said yes. I was so excited. It was almost midnight, and I called and woke up all my friends with the great news. About three weeks after our engagement, Luke wanted to see my divorce papers. I looked at the date of the filing and realized my ex had filed for divorce on April 3, 1998, three years to the day Luke proposed to me!

The next morning, when Luke came to pick me up for work, we prayed about when we should marry. The Lord spoke to us at the same time in our spirits and told us June. That was wild because several months before Luke and I ever met, I was at a prophetic meeting in Mobile, Alabama, and Bob Jones got up and said he felt some people in the room were going to get married in June. When he said that, I felt a strong witness in my spirit. I never told Luke about that until after we had both heard from the Lord about June. When I went to talk to my pastor he was not quite as thrilled as we were about the engagement. In fact, my pastor asked me to put the engagement on the back burner and not to tell anyone how God put Luke and I together, and not to tell anyone in the congregation we were engaged. I was crushed! My mom also was not happy with the union and would not help with the wedding and even told me that one of my brothers could not attend because he was in college taking finals. When Luke and I went to my parents' house one day, my step-dad was on the phone with my brother, so I got the phone from him while my mom was in the bathroom. My brother told me he knew I was engaged but didn't know the wedding was next weekend. He also told me that Mom knew all of his finals were already over and she also knew that he was planning to come home that weekend anyway with his girlfriend. I quickly invited him, his girlfriend and all of his friends to the wedding. During one of my phone conversations with my mom about my wedding, I let Luke listen in and he could not believe a mother would say some of the things that she did to her own daughter. Luke and I felt like the entire world was coming against us so we prayed earnestly for God's intervention.

In case you are wondering why our pastor wasn't supportive at first, I think it was probably because Luke told him originally he was going to marry someone else. Plus, after the congregation found out, three people went to our pastor and told him that God had spoken to them and said our marriage was not of God. Luke had been in that church almost his entire Christian walk and had been taught you needed the pastor's permission to marry someone and that you had to be in complete submission to his authority.

Our pastor and Luke's mentor insisted that we could not marry for two years. *I* knew that was wrong because Luke and I had already consulted the Lord and He told both of us June. I also knew there was nowhere in the Bible that stated it was the pastor's call on who you could or could not marry and when. I prayed for God's intervention again because Luke refused to stand his ground with our pastor. Luke and I were at our church's pre-marital counseling which was taught by a wonderful couple, Clint and Roseanne, who were a big help in putting our wedding together. At the end of one of the sessions, a missionary who was staying at their house, and did not know what was going on, gave us a word from the Lord telling us that if God told us to get married and we were dragging our feet, then we were in disobedience and we were stalling the destiny God had for us. That was enough of a warning for Luke! He informed Roseanne immediately we were setting a date and the next day he was in the pastor's office, and this time he wasn't taking no for an answer. We were to be married on July 7, 2001. It was too late for June because of Luke's disobedience. Never choose man over God!

Now we really started praying. We had no extra money, barely enough to cover bills, and were to be married in about three weeks. Then, a miracle! Luke's parents generously gave us $5,000. That was a huge amount of money to them and definitely not expected.

I had previously prayed for a trip to Puerto Vallarta, Mexico, and one day at work, a lady I barely knew asked me where I was going on my honeymoon. I told her I would like to go to Puerto Vallarta, and she said, "Really? I have a timeshare there with some extra weeks. Would you like to use it?" I did not have to think twice about that one. It was a beautiful two-bedroom facing the beach with a hot tub on the deck in a big, gorgeous resort. Our pastor let us use the church for free, and Luke's mentor offered to perform the ceremony for free.

Luke and I went together to look at cakes and the one I wanted was about $1,500, and the groom's cake was around $500. I left very gloomy because we could not even come close to buying them. All the money we were given had to cover other expenses. Oh well, we just made the best of it. Rosanne later offered to organize our entire wedding for free, and she even donated the flowers! Wow, talk about a godsend! Then Roseanne called me and said her friend, a caterer, had an extra wedding cake from a wedding that never happened and would I like to see it? I told her I did not have to see it; I would happily take it. Rosanne told me she and her husband would also get us a groom's cake! I was so thankful! On my wedding day, when I was getting ready, I looked through a little window in the bride's room at the cake, and I could not believe my eyes! It was the same wedding cake I had wanted at the wedding bakery! We serve an awesome God! Then, during the wedding, one of the gentlemen from our church was walking around with a big fancy camera; he was a professional photographer who not only took the pictures, but gave them to us for free with frames!

Something I had not mentioned till now—part of the money that was spent went to plane fare. One night, Luke was researching prices on a website that auctioned plane tickets. He was trying to find the going prices for the tickets we wanted. One of our friends told us that splitting our flight to stop at Mexico City on the way to Puerto Vallarta was the least expensive way to go. Luke wanted to see if this was true, so he put in some bids he thought were way lower than the company would accept, so they would then let him know he lost the bid, and that the fares were currently going for a certain price.

About a week before the wedding, we went to pull some money out of Luke's account, and some money was missing! We looked at the transaction: the company had accepted Luke's bid. We had great tickets to Mexico City, but no tickets to Puerto Vallarta! What a mess, but we just put it in God's hands and went on with other preparations. At the last minute, my mom came around, and the night of the wedding, my parents rented us a limo and threw us a small family party at their house afterwards. During the party they gave us $1,500! This was more than enough to cover the extra plane fare to Puerto Vallarta for our honeymoon. I also have to mention that a beautiful young couple rented us a room at a nearby hotel as a wedding gift for our first night together. They covered the bed and floor with rose petals; it was so beautiful! We left for Mexico on our honeymoon the next morning.

God brought together our entire wedding in three weeks! When I was lying in Luke's arms during our honeymoon, the Lord spoke to me in that still small voice and said, "Do you know why you like your wedding ring so much?" For years I had looked at wedding rings and had always wanted a band with a tri-gold rope that was intertwined. That is what we bought for our wedding rings.

"Why, Lord?"

"Because a three-braided cord is not easily broken" (Ecc. 4:12, NLT). That was the scripture Luke had been standing on for his mate for several years! I am more in love with my husband today than when we first married, and I look forward to spending a lifetime with him.

LUKE'S TESTIMONY

By now you have heard my wife's side of our story. Mine is different, but God demonstrates Himself no less faithfully. The story truly needs to start with my growing up because I was pretty normal for the most part; perhaps this relates to you.

I grew up in small-town Texas with one twin brother, sons of an ex-army sergeant/oil man and a mom who was a high school teacher/counselor. My parents loved me and did their very best to protect me from the hurtful things in life. They did a pretty good job; I was very sheltered and had no idea people could be mean to one another. Don't get me wrong, Dad loved me and would sell his soul for us, but the hard life he had growing up came out when he was angry. My brother and I just did our best not to make him too mad and to stay away when he had been drinking. He was an alcoholic;

he drank a lot, and when he drank, which was pretty much all the time, he had a tendency to be verbally abusive. Other than that, life was good.

Our mom was great. Life was fun and pretty much carefree for us. I didn't know it, but we didn't have much money. My brother had been very sick as a baby. His heart was too big for his chest, and one lung was not functional, and his spine was twisted so badly he later had a steel rod put in his back. As a result, he stayed in a glass box the first year of his life. The week he got out, he contracted bronchitis which turned into pneumonia, which put him right back into the hospital. The hospital bills were astronomical, and my mom and dad did their best to pay. Then we hit the oil crunch in the '80s with home interest rates doubling overnight and people out of work everywhere. Living in Houston was pretty tough. Because of the enormous overhead that my parents had to endure with the hospital bills, they made the best of things, and we moved from our home in a nice subdivision to a beautiful little boat on Clear Lake with about 300 square feet of living space. That was fun. My parents partied all the time, and I grew up listening to '50s music and Jimmy Buffett. It was burgers in paradise for real. My brother and I were the envy of every kid we knew, so we didn't even notice that we didn't have some of the stuff other kids had.

My mom and dad went to great lengths to protect us from bad people, and that had a big influence in our lives. To my mom and dad, this meant no church and no belief in God. I was quite proud of them. They told me as a little boy that they would not go to church, but when I was old enough to make my own decision, I could go then. We celebrated Christmas and sang all the carols; I had no idea what any of that stuff meant. I think that happened after my best friend asked me at school one day what church I went to. I remember it like it was yesterday. Rex asked where I went to church, and I said I didn't. I wasn't defensive; I didn't know that was a bad thing. Then Rex became very mean, and said I must be "one of those agnostics or atheists." I went home and asked my parents what an atheist was, and they asked what happened. I think that is where the church conversation came from. That was my only exposure to church people. Please note the damage that did to my life. Rex's comment was learned at home, and it only deepened the offense my parents had with the church. Be very careful to coach your children on how to show Christ's love.

Years later, after I had gone through high school drinking and attempting to sleep around to be cool (all my parent protectiveness left me completely inept when it came to girls), I did my undergrad at the University of Houston. I had absolutely no idea what I wanted to do with my life, so I went for engineering because I was good at math and knew engineers made money. I also enrolled in marching band because I was a percussionist, and I truly loved playing in drumlines. I learned a lot during this time, and knew even less than I thought I did. My parents just laughed at me, because like all college students, I thought I knew everything.

I want to make a side note here. I mentioned earlier that my dad was an ex-Army sarge. He was an exceptional leader in the Army and was very successful there, but it had a couple of downsides at home. The yelling for one (children just are not meant to handle that), and me being told what to do in every single area of my life. It may not have been that extreme—it seemed like it was—and I definitely resented being told what to do to that extent. As I went into music, I was also told what to do in excruciating detail. The key point is that I have had to work through being groomed to take directions from others, with my own opinions not being valid. If I didn't like it, it didn't matter. If I disagreed, it didn't matter. So when I chose to go to church, it was really one of the first times I followed my instinct.

Let me tell you, that decision was not well received at home. My parents were trying to protect me; they had only been hurt by the church. My dad was raised in the Great Depression, and his father died when he was about ten. Then he and his mother moved in with Grandma, and she tried to make it in real estate. I am still amazed by this, but some clergy member stole from my grandma, and it really hurt them financially. They had a hard time supporting themselves after that. I suspect that offense is why they left the Catholic Church. Offense is dangerous! That event changed my dad's life, possibly forever. Please be careful to honor God in what you say and do. Please do the best you can to not give or hold on to offense. Later, my grandma contracted cancer, and my dad rode railroad cars all over the U.S.

trying to find a cure to help her. He rode all the way to Chicago, got some medicine, brought it back, and she still died. Then later my dad's older brother choked to death on a piece of steak in front of the whole family. Can you imagine? My dad had buried his entire family by the time he was about twenty-five. He never talked about any of it; this information I got from my mom. Then there was my mom. Her dad died when she was a girl. In both cases, they wondered how a loving God would allow those things to happen. It was tragic, but they never bothered to find a different answer than the ones they had created.

In the fall of my sophomore year at the University of Houston, I met Matt. By this time I had switched my major to music education and was moving into Bates Hall, which apparently was famous at U of H. As I opened the door of my new room, the wall just inside the door was lined with about twelve pairs of muddy athletic shoes, all the same size, each one apparently for a different purpose. I was living with a jock? Oh no! This was going to be horrible! I didn't meet him until I came home from practicing that night. Matt is now a preacher, and we have joked frequently that whoever has the microphone wins, and right now, I've got it.

Matt was 6'4", about 180 pounds, and had a grin from ear to ear. He was done with his workout for the day, he plopped down on his bed, and his first words after "Hi, I'm Matt" were, "So do ya like to drink a lot of beer?" (Sorry, Matt, I couldn't resist!) Then he proceeded to pull out an igloo chest from under his bed; it was full of cheap beer. Not even good beer! I, of course, in an attempt to be friendly, accepted his offer. We got along great. That semester was interesting. Matt was a decathlete, and my girlfriend was completely enamored by him. I thought that was pretty funny. I was totally unsaved, and Matt had been to church but didn't know Christ at all. God began to work on Matt's heart that semester. He was on his way to the Olympics, and the U of H track coaches were some of the best in the world.

Matt began to read the Bible on Sundays. I thought that was ridiculous and tried to make light of the situation. One evening I came home and he was reading the Bible again. Then I said something that really freaked him out. The frames for the mattresses that were in the dorms were really squeaky, so I put my mattress on the floor and Matt kept his mattress on his bed frame. It happened that we had colored lights at each of our desks on opposite sides of the room. Matt's was blue, which was illuminated by my red light. I walked in the door, and almost without thought, I said, "Hey, Matt, look! Heaven..." (pointing at his side of the room) "and hell!" (pointing at my side of the room). I wish you could have seen the look on his face. He didn't look up from his Bible for the next three days. I thought it was hilarious. I guess I freaked him out so much that he decided to move out at the end of that semester. (I think he wanted to move in with a friend from his track team.)

During the next two years, I made friends with

two guys, both of whom were Christians. Every time I would talk with Raymond alone, for some reason I wanted to know about God. We would pray, and I would tell him that I wasn't going to give my life to God. Donnie, who played with me in the drumline, told me later he joined that drumline because he felt God had sent him there to share the gospel. His sharing worked, because out of eight guys, two are now preachers, one converted from Judaism to Christianity, and the other guys felt really convicted all year. I was impressed. Two years later, in the fall of 1994 when I was finishing school, it should have been an exciting time to be alive. However, I was losing my enthusiasm for life. I had a lot of things going for me: I was doing very well in my school, and I was one of the top percussionists. But I was still feeling really empty inside. I was ending a long relationship with a girl, and was really torn up about it. I was partying heavily with my fraternity—which basically meant I drank a lot of beer—so I was looking for something but I didn't know what. I thought I was a good person because I was always faithful to my girlfriends and never did drugs. (I had friends in other frats who had no idea how many girlfriends they had. How horrible is that?) Again, I was looking for something and that something found me.

I was starting the education phase of my coursework, finishing up my music education degree. I was quite fortunate in that there was a young man who knew me from marching band, and I guess he thought I was cool. I had no idea who he was, but I am eternally thankful to him. His name was BJ, and he decided he wanted to be my friend. To him, being friends meant going to church together. He was quite persistent, and fortunately for me, he was also quite resourceful. I took full advantage of our relationship. He did papers for me and whatever else I could think of. I was a real jerk. But every week it was, "Luke, why don't you come to church with me on Sunday?" Every Sunday I would turn him down.

Finally, I started doing other things that scared me. The morals I held in certain areas of my life began to decay. I decided I needed a change, but I still wasn't sure what. BJ invited me to church again, and I very painfully consented. Before I knew it, I was introduced to a whole new people group. Christians! Boy, there were a lot of them. BJ took me to Second Baptist Church in Houston, and I was impressed. The people were so nice, and the girls were pretty good looking, but I behaved because they were Christians.

BJ took me to church for the next six weeks on Sundays, and I eventually began to visit the Friday night social thing they had, too. Those people began to remember my name, and I really liked it there. The Sunday school teachers were really nice, and it seemed like a perfect world. Then came the preaching. Dr. Young could sure preach, and I listened. At the end of every service, he would give an altar call, and I would feel this weird gut-wrenching pain in my stomach and would break into a sweat, and (without knowing what I was doing), I would tell God, "I just can't do it" very quietly. Then the Sunday before my twenty-second birthday (up to this point, my mom and dad had no idea; I made up some excuse to always be away on Sundays), I woke up suddenly. I was completely awake, and I said out loud, "Today, I am giving my life to Christ." Ask my wife—me waking up suddenly is a miracle in and of itself.

I went to church that day and just listened in Sunday school. When it was time to go to big church, I made the entire Sunday school sit on the same pew beside me, so I was on the end. That was about sixty people. I didn't want to give myself any excuse to talk myself out of going up to the front when the altar call was given. It worked. I just waited for the sermon to be over, and the second he started going into the altar call, I stood up and marched straight down to the stage in front of about 6,000 people. It didn't occur to me that I was alone and that Dr. Young had just preached a sermon to married women about sex. Wow. Anyway, as I waited for Dr. Young to finish the altar call, I walked back where they told me to go. Someone got a real lesson in humility that day; it wasn't me. I didn't find out what the message was until about two years later after I researched the church's records. Who says God doesn't have a sense of humor?

Last story, I promise. As I went to the back after I answered the altar call, they told me to sit down opposite some big guy in a suit. Keep in mind that I was a music major and had never watched sports, except football. I certainly didn't keep up with anybody's name.

It turned out that the guy was some famous baseball player for the Astros. I didn't know who he was. I guess he could tell, because as I sat down, he stood up and said, "Hi, I'm John Smith [*name changed*]."

And I said, "Nice to meet you, Mr. Smith."

He didn't get the reaction he was looking for, because he said his name again. That was weird. "Hi, I'm John Smith."

"Nice to meet you, Mr. Smith."

I was still clueless, and by now I thought this guy needed a clue. He kind of paused, shrugged his huge shoulders, and plunged into explaining the tract was he was giving me. After he prayed with me, he just couldn't let go of the fact I had no idea who he was. He went for it again, "Hi, I'm John Smith."

"Thank you, Mr. Smith, it was nice to meet you," I said. He couldn't believe I didn't know him, and I couldn't figure out what was with this guy. I saw his name later on TV and just laughed.

The next weekend I went to visit my parents and I knew I was going to have to get out of helping the family on Sunday so I could go to church. On Saturday, I asked if I could leave the next day to go to church. I had never seen my dad so angry; he asked me who I had been talking to. When I told him I became a Christian, it was World War Three in the middle of our front lawn! Here was my dad, who I respected, ripping me apart and condemning me for attending church. He was hurt, because he knew he was losing me, and I was so special to him. He had fun watching me go out and drink and carouse with women. He thought that was what I should be doing, and here I was ditching a lifestyle he approved, and running right into the arms of the organization he perceived had hurt him and his family. (He had never read the Bible or knew what it said.)

Over the course of the next few years, my relationship with my parents steadily worsened, always coming back to the fact that I was now a Pentecostal. It took me some time to learn what a Pentecostal was. I graduated from the University of Houston with a degree in music education, and went on to obtain a master's degree in music performance from Rice University. I was well on my way to a solid career as a musician. I looked good on paper, and I played well, but all the discord with my parents had taken its toll. I would rather practice than socialize, so I resorted to being arrogant with people to keep them at arm's length. I loved teaching kids, so I had no problems there, probably because kids weren't a threat to me. My life consisted of attending church, practicing music, music rehearsals, and teaching music privately as a clinician. I didn't have many friends, and that was fine with me because it gave me more time to practice. During these years of study, and shortly afterwards, I was disowned as a son twice by my parents because of my refusal to stop attending church. Finally, I had to cut off my parents because they never accepted my wife because she was a Christian. At the time of this writing, I have seen more bad things in people than I ever wanted to. It's just hard to understand why people can be so hurtful.

The basic premise was that my parents were supportive on the surface. They gave us help financially when we needed help once and were very supportive with our wedding, above and beyond what they had to do, but in their hearts, they resented Bethany. They tried to make her feel unwelcome, hoping we would get a divorce. My dad actually told me not to get her pregnant because I would be forced to stay married to her. That was one of the last conversations we ever had. After that, I decided I would not subject myself or my wife to their abuse any longer. I wrote them a very detailed email, confiding in them how I felt, but my mom wrote back stating that they refused to back off their stance concerning my wife or my relationship with God. Bethany and I have not seen them since. One of the things that God taught me was how to recognize safe and unsafe people and how to deal with them even if they are your parents. Just because you are related to someone does not mean they have a right to abuse you and that you have to subject yourself to their abuse.

I included all this information to give you some of my background so it might possibly encourage you, as well as give you some insight into why I handled myself in certain ways when I worked with Bethany. After I became a Christian, I really had no idea how to talk to a Christian girl and was pretty poor at relating to people. I was used to being told what to do and how to think—first by my dad, then by my teachers, and when I went to church, by my spiritual mentor. Unfortunately, some of the relationships in my church went a bit too far when they would "speak into my life." Once again, I was being frequently told what to do, and I was right back at square one.

The last relationship I had with a young lady before Bethany occurred while I was a senior at the University of Houston. She was wonderful. I met her at Second Baptist where I committed my life to Christ. (I only attended Second Baptist for about six months, when later I went with my old roommate Matt to his church. That church is where Bethany and I met.) I will simply state that my relationship with this young lady ended, and a big reason for that was my own pride, arrogance, and a poor attitude. (I can hear all the women now, "Did I date *him?*") At the end of that relationship, I determined to spend time simply allowing God to mature me and that my next girlfriend would be my wife. I chose not to date until I met the woman I was sure was going to be my wife. I would not recommend this to anyone, but I know this is what God did for me.

I met Bethany for the first time about six years later. I was twenty-seven, single, and very involved in my church. The young adults ministry held a Bible study at my town home, and I worked till about 7 PM at the time, so one night when I showed up late to the Bible study, Bethany was there, crammed up on the end of my couch right by the door. When I walked in, it was hard not to notice her. She was so beautiful I caught my breath when I laid eyes on her. She had the most gorgeous hair I had ever seen. She was obviously uncomfortable being there, so I left her alone except for a few stolen glances when I thought she wasn't looking.

Now the story really gets interesting because of a few decisions I made, most of which I would never recommend to anyone. In my college ministry, I had watched people going through a lot of drama while single, believing God was putting them together with this person or with that person. I was never willing to spend much time dwelling on relationships, so I asked God to make me the last person to know when it was time for me to get married. He answered my prayer. Most of my story, and the pain it caused Bethany during that year, is a result of that answered prayer and my pride. As I look back, some of it was pretty funny. Bethany still isn't laughing though!

As you will remember from the previous chapter, God spoke to Bethany about me in a prayer meeting. Please keep in mind that in theory, I was the leader of the prayer ministry at church and didn't even have a fundamental biblical understanding of how to pray. Bethany, of course, did, and she very quickly realized I was not scripturally sound in this area. My ignorance was only exceeded by my pride, and Bethany found that out quickly as she tried to offer me some advice. What makes this funnier is that I was still a person who genuinely loved God as much as I knew how, so God honored that and helped me be a blessing to people as I prayed for them.

After I had offended Bethany by rudely dismissing her attempt to educate me on how to pray, I asked if I could pray for her. In a supreme display of insensitivity, I told her I suspected she had trust issues. I wish you could have seen the look on her face: it makes me smile just thinking of it. At that point, I continued to pray, and then something very interesting happened. I could actually see what I could only describe as a halo over her head. I could see it as clear as day. I somehow knew she was definitely in Houston to get married. I really go out of my way to not be super-spiritual as some would call it, and stuff like this had never happened to me, so I was amazed at what I was seeing. I described what I saw to the eight or so people in attendance that night. I had no idea that the Holy Spirit was trying to get through to me. God is very patient and merciful.

When I met Bethany, I was working in real estate. Yes, I know, what happened to music? God is faithful there too, and I am working on that right now, but at the time I was selling homes. That was one way God was forcing me to learn about talking to people. Ouch, what a lesson.

Once Bethany moved back to Houston, God went about His business to get us together. In most cases, I believe God will develop a relationship between two people so that they can begin the process of smoothing off the rough edges while they are getting to know one another. My church had an unwritten but spoken rule of no dating and discouraged young men and women from forming close relationships. This is probably why most of those people did not get married until they were older, and for the most part, were frustrated.

After I had left my job, my spiritual mentor asked me to work for him in his company. I was also interested in finance, so I worked at another company part time to learn. God had an interesting way around the no-dating rule. Before I knew what was happening, both Bethany and I ended up working at the same company during the day, and she worked at the same finance company part time. Bethany had no idea I was working at the finance company. After she was hired by both companies, I was asked by both companies to train Bethany in a few areas. We had to spend a lot of time together.

It was during this time that I began to get to know Bethany. She began to share her dreams and the hopes she had for the future. What was so alarming to me was that we had very similar hopes and dreams in some very specific areas, not general areas like having children or working in this career field or that career field, but specific things that matched exactly. I was terrified. I knew it was no mistake that this woman was in my life and shared the same vision I did for the future. Whenever I had heard of anything like this happening before, it was always a precursor to marriage. I was so used to my life that the prospect of my life changing significantly made me very uncomfortable. I did not feel at all ready for marriage. I felt I had way too much baggage and not enough financial stability! God apparently believed in His ability to change me more than I did.

We fought a lot. She wasted no time in pulling apart false biblical doctrines I held to be true. It was no fun. I had never met anyone before who had so much knowledge of the Bible and knew how to present it so it made sense. She didn't use rules from our church. Bethany would open the Word of God and show me how the Bible addressed practical issues in life. If you have never read the Bible, you need to do that on your own and not just let yourself be spoon-fed by others. You will not know if what someone is telling you is true if you have not studied the Word of God.

What was really confusing about Bethany was that I already thought I knew who my wife was, but wasn't sure. It was another young lady. I too had gotten caught up in the who-is-my-wife game I had been trying to avoid. On top of that, I was not physically or emotionally attracted to the other girl, but I was very attracted to Bethany. I had known the other girl for a few years, and she was sweet enough. I don't care to go into all the details because it is sad I was so foolish and easily deceived. I simply had a dream, or perhaps a vision, that seemed alarmingly real to me. It was this girl in my dream, nothing inappropriate, but I thought God was pointing her out as my wife. To make matters worse, it seemed she and I would run into each other at odd times, and those did not seem like coincidence. This furthered my belief she might be my wife.

I had no concept of what it meant to be led by the

Spirit of God because I was allowing myself to be led by men, because that is how I was raised. I did not pursue the other young lady aggressively because I was not sure, so I waited to see if God would work things out. I did go and tell my pastor and mentor about her, which I later regretted. Be careful putting your faith in dreams. God speaks to us through dreams sometimes, but this one was not from Him. You have to cultivate a personal relationship with God through Christ and learn to hear from Him on a personal level. I also found out later that this lady was never interested in me at all. It was very hard for Bethany because, while I was attracted to her physically and in my heart, I had this conflict that the other young lady might be my wife. I was very confused.

Shortly after I recognized Bethany was special, I realized I was wrong, and the other young lady left the picture. I was still nervous about Bethany and the real prospect of marriage. Something that God did to clear this up for me was one evening, we drove to my parents' home to get my twin brother and take him out to a movie. While riding with Bethany in the car, I had such joy in my spirit, just being with her, that I knew God was trying to let me know. I also knew I could not fabricate this joy; it was definitely supernatural. Then late one afternoon, while we were hanging out in a bookstore, I fell in love with Bethany and wanted to spend the rest of my life with her. I will never forget that moment. I knew she was the one.

I was still fearful, so I held her at arm's length. Additionally, I had told my spiritual mentor I wanted to marry her and asked him what to do. He told me to put it on the shelf because it was probably just lust. This meant I was to stay away from Bethany and not speak with her intimately. I longed to be with her but was afraid that if I disobeyed my mentor, I would be disobeying God. This caused a lot of confusion in my friendship with Bethany because I would flirt with her, then my mentor's voice would pop in my head about lust and I would be mean to her. After a while, I realized that putting our relationship on the shelf was not correct. I was driving in my car, and I told God I was ditching every rule I had ever learned in the church about women because none of them had ever worked and I knew it was His will that I marry Bethany. I flirted shamelessly with her at a friend's birthday party that evening and did not care who noticed. The rest is history...

One last note: I think it would be well said that a key indicator to the will of God is peace. Colossians 3:15 (TAB) states, "And let the peace (soul harmony which comes) from Christ rule (act as umpire continually) in your hearts [deciding and settling with finality all questions that arise in your minds, in that peaceful state] to which as [members of Christ's] one body you were also called [to live]..." The day of our wedding, I could have been dropping off my dry cleaning for as nervous as I was, which is a backwards way of saying that I wasn't nervous at all. My groomsmen and future father-in-law kept asking if I was nervous, and I replied, "No, not at all." I had complete peace. Bethany is the love of my life and my very best friend.

WHAT ABOUT HOMOSEXUALITY?

I hear a lot of confusion on the subject of homosexuality today, about whether it is a sin or not. Also, I know that people want to know if marriage is really the union between one man and one woman. If you are a Christian, then your answers to life's questions need to be found in the Word of God.

Let's start by reading from Genesis chapters one and two:

> And God said, Let us make man in our image, after our likeness: and let them have dominion over the fish of the sea, and over the fowl of the air, and over the cattle, and over all the earth, and over every creeping thing that creepeth upon the earth. *So God created man in his own image, in the image of God*

created he him; male and female created he them. And
God blessed them, and God said unto them, Be fruit-
ful, and multiply, and replenish the earth, and sub-
due it: and have dominion over the fish of the sea,
and over the fowl of the air, and over every living
thing that moveth upon the earth. And God said,
Behold, I have given you every herb bearing seed,
which is upon the face of all the earth, and every
tree, in the which is the fruit of a tree yielding seed;
to you it shall be for meat.

Genesis 1:26–29 (KJV)

As you can see, God created man and woman to
"increase in number." Two men together, or two
women together cannot "increase in number" in the
natural way God intended.

And out of the ground the LORD God formed every
beast of the field, and every fowl of the air; and
brought them unto Adam to see what he would
call them: and whatsoever Adam called every living creature, that was the name thereof. And Adam
gave names to all cattle, and to the fowl of the air,
and to every beast of the field; *but for Adam there*
was not found an help meet for him. And the LORD
God caused a deep sleep to fall upon Adam, and he
slept: and he took one of his ribs, and closed up the
flesh instead thereof; And the rib, which the LORD *God*
had taken from man, made he a woman, and brought

her unto the man. And Adam said, This is now bone of my bones, and flesh of my flesh: she shall be called Woman, because she was taken out of Man. Therefore shall a man leave his father and his mother, and shall cleave unto his wife: and they shall be one flesh. And they were both naked, the man and his wife, and were not ashamed.

Genesis 2:19–25 (KJV)

Again, we realize in the above scripture that God only wanted a woman to be a man's wife. God actually created the woman out of part of the man and when a man and woman get married, they become one flesh and are able to increase in number. Read next what Apostle Paul writes to Timothy:

...wanting to be teachers of the Law, even though they do not understand either what they are saying or the matters about which they make confident assertions. *But we know that the Law is good, if one uses it lawfully, realizing the fact that law is not made for a righteous person, but for those who are lawless and rebellious, for the ungodly and sinners, for the unholy and profane, for those who kill their fathers or mothers, for murderers and immoral men and homosexuals and kidnappers and liars and perjurers, and whatever else is contrary to sound teaching,* according to the glorious gospel of the blessed God, with which I have been entrusted.

1 Timothy 1:7–11 (NASB)

Paul teaches Timothy that homosexuality is *"contrary to sound teaching."* In 1 Corinthians, Paul states that homosexuals will not inherit nor have any share in the kingdom of God:

> Do you not know that the unrighteous and the wrongdoers will not inherit or have any share in the kingdom of God? *Do not be deceived (misled): neither the impure and immoral, nor idolaters, nor adulterers, nor those who participate in homosexuality, Nor cheats (swindlers and thieves), nor greedy graspers, nor drunkards, nor foulmouthed revilers and slanderers, nor extortioners and robbers will inherit or have any share in the kingdom of God.*
>
> 1 Corinthians 6:9–10 (TAB)

Romans Chapter one is one of the most famous passages that Paul wrote about homosexuality:

> Therefore God gave them up in the lusts of their [own] hearts to sexual impurity, to the dishonoring of their bodies among themselves [abandoning them to the degrading power of sin], because they exchanged the truth of God for a lie and worshiped and served the creature rather than the Creator, Who is blessed forever! Amen (so be it). *For this reason God gave them over and abandoned them to vile affections and degrading passions. For their women exchanged their natural function for an unnatural and abnormal one, And the men also turned from nat-*

ural relations with women and were set ablaze (burn-ing out, consumed) with lust for one another—men committing shameful acts with men and suffering in their own bodies and personalities the inevitable con-sequences and penalty of their wrong-doing and going astray, which was [their] fitting retribution. And so, since they did not see fit to acknowledge God or approve of Him or consider Him worth the know-ing, God gave them over to a base and condemned mind to do things not proper or decent but loath-some, Until they were filled (permeated and satu-rated) with every kind of unrighteousness, iniquity, grasping and covetous greed, and malice. [They were] full of envy and jealousy, murder, strife, deceit and treachery, ill will and cruel ways. [They were] secret backbiters and gossipers, Slanderers, hateful to and hating God, full of insolence, arrogance, [and] boasting; inventors of new forms of evil, dis-obedient and undutiful to parents. [They were] without understanding, conscienceless and faith-less, heartless and loveless [and] merciless. Though they are fully aware of God's righteous decree that those who do such things deserve to die, they not only do them themselves but approve and applaud others who practice them.

Romans 1:24–32 (TAB)

Please notice Paul writes in Romans chapter one that the people knew the right thing to do, but *chose* not to do it. Paul also calls homosexuality a *vile* affection. Homosexuality is a sin, and according to God's Word, it is a choice. I was praying with a friend a few years ago, and the Lord revealed to me that she had a demonic spirit of homosexuality. I asked her if she had ever been involved in that practice and she said, "No, never."

I asked the Lord what was going on and He responded, *"Anyone who practices any type of sex sin opens a door for any type of spirit to walk in that wants to, including homosexuality."* That's right, the Holy Spirit is just that, holy, and He will never lead you into sin. Anything compelling you towards sin is not the Holy Spirit but an ungodly one. Satan works through your soul, which is your mind and your emotions. God is a spirit and He communicates with your spirit. You must train your spirit by prayer, reading God's Word, and obeying Him. You can receive freedom from homosexuality through the power of God, but the Holy Spirit's power must be a reality in your life to stay free from all sin. I also want to note here that as Christians, we are not the judge of unbelievers, God is, so please walk in love towards all people whether or not you agree with their lifestyle. However, if someone claims to be a Christian and is in immorality you are not supposed to associate with them. Paul explains this in 1 Corinthians below:

> I wrote you in my letter not to associate with
> immoral people; I did not at all mean with the

immoral people of this world, or with the covetous and swindlers, or with idolaters, for then you would have to go out of the world. But actually, I wrote to you not to associate with any so-called brother if he is an immoral person, or covetous, or an idolater, or a reviler, or a drunkard, or a swindler—not even to eat with such a one. For what have I to do with judging outsiders? Do you not judge those who are within the church? But those who are outside, God judges. *Remove the wicked man from among yourselves.*

> 1 Corinthians 5:9–13 (NASB)

Here are a few scriptures that reveal to you God's will on how you should live:

> *For this is the will of God, even your sanctification, that ye should abstain from fornication:* That every one of you should know how to possess his vessel in sanctification and honor.
>
> 1 Thessalonians 4:3–4 (KJV)

Notice that it is God's will that you should avoid fornication. If you are in sexual sin, you are *out of God's will!*

> For as many as have sinned without law shall also perish without law: and as many as have sinned in the law shall be judged by the law; (For not the hearers of the law are just before God, but the doers

of the law shall be justified. For when the Gentiles, which have not the law, do by nature the things contained in the law, these, having not the law, are a law unto themselves: Which shew the work of the law written in their hearts, their conscience also bearing witness, and their thoughts the mean while accusing or else excusing one another;) In the day when God shall judge the secrets of men by Jesus Christ according to my gospel.

Romans 2:12–16 (KJV)

God's Word states that our conscience already knows right from wrong. What is your conscience telling you? How are we to deal with sexual sin? Flee from it! If you are in the sin of homosexuality and want out, you have to be willing to admit it is sin, repent before God, forgive others who have hurt you, and take a strong, active stand against all sin. Jesus said in Mark 11:25–26, "*And when ye stand praying, forgive, if ye have ought against any: that your Father also which is in heaven may forgive you your trespasses. But if ye do not forgive, neither will your Father which is in heaven forgive your trespasses.*"

Transgression means sins, so for you to be forgiven of your sins, you must forgive others. Forgiveness simply means not holding what someone else did to you against them. So I have included that you must forgive those who have hurt you in this prayer. If you are ready to be free from homosexuality, please pray the following prayer out loud and be very sincere in your heart:

Dear Lord,

I know that homosexuality is a sin, and I choose to stop. I am asking for Your divine intervention so I can be completely free from all sin, including sexual sin. I choose to forgive everyone who has ever hurt me and I ask that You now forgive me of every sin I have ever committed including homosexuality. I ask that You wash away my sins with the blood of Your Son Jesus Christ. I believe in my heart and I confess with my mouth that Your Son Jesus Christ walked this earth in the flesh, died on a cross for my sins, rose again three days later, and now sits at Your right hand (Romans 10:9–10). This Jesus is now my Lord and Savior, and I am born again (John 3:3–5). Father God, I am Yours now, please fill me with Your Holy Spirit. Satan, I take authority over you and the spirit of homosexuality, and I command you to leave me now and forever in Jesus' name (Luke 10:19). I ask that the Holy Spirit would now bring order to my life and to my steps. Please reveal Your plan and purpose for my life and place me in the church family You have for me. Thank You, in Your Son Jesus' name, amen.

WALKING IN HOLINESS

The LORD reigneth, he is clothed with majesty; the LORD is clothed with strength, wherewith he hath girded himself: the world also is stablished, that it cannot be moved. Thy throne is established of old: thou art from everlasting. The floods have lifted up, O LORD, the floods have lifted up their voice; the floods lift up their waves. The LORD on high is mightier than the noise of many waters, yea, than the mighty waves of the sea. Thy testimonies are very sure: holiness becometh thine house, O LORD, for ever.

Psalm 93 (KJV)

A life of holiness is about living a sold-out life to doing the Lord's will for your life. So how do you know the Lord's will concerning sex before marriage? You read His Word that He gave all of us to live by. As you can already imagine, Luke and I did not consummate our marriage till our wedding night. Since I was previously married and very wild even before that, I was not a virgin by any stretch of the imagination. I still knew it was best to obey God the second time around and wait. Luke did too. So even if you have been promiscuous, it is never too late to start making the right choice. If someone really does love and care about you, they will wait. When God gives us rules to live by, it is to protect us. When we obey Him and wait until marriage to have sex, we avoid sexual diseases (assuming you both waited!), not as many broken hearts and pains of rejection, and fewer unwanted pregnancies. Can you think of any more? The list could go on. When you sin, you turn your God-given authority over to Satan by your own free will. There is actually power in holiness. Remember, God is holy and He is all-powerful. Sin separates you from God. Why do you think Satan tries so hard to get people to sin? So he can take away their authority over him. Do you see how God wants to protect you from getting hurt? When you love someone, don't you want to protect them? God loves you, so He sets up rules to protect you like parents set up rules to protect their children. You are God's child! I list several New Testament scriptures; please read and consider the implications of not obeying God's Holy Word concerning sex.

...Know ye not that the unrighteous shall not inherit the kingdom of God? Be not deceived: neither fornicators, nor idolaters, nor adulterers, nor effeminate, nor abusers of themselves with mankind, nor thieves, nor covetous, nor drunkards, nor revilers, nor extortioners, shall inherit the kingdom of God.

1 Corinthians 6:9–10 (KJV)

Flee fornication. Every sin that a man doeth is without the body; but he that committeth fornication sinneth against his own body. What? Know ye not that your body is the temple of the Holy Ghost which is in you, which ye have of God, and ye are not your own? *For ye are bought with a price: therefore glorify God in your body, and in your spirit, which are God's.*

1 Corinthians 6:18–20 (KJV)

Away then with sinful, earthly things; deaden the evil desires lurking within you; *have nothing to do with sexual sin, impurity, lust and shameful desires;* don't worship the good things of life, for that is idolatry. *God's terrible anger is upon those who do such things.*

Colossians 3:5–6 (TLB)

Marriage is honorable in all, and the bed undefiled: but whoremongers and adulterers God will judge.

Hebrews 13:4 (KJV)

Thou shalt not commit adultery

Exodus 20 (commandment 7)

Hebrew—*zanah, zaw-naw';* means adultery, fornication, and idolatry.
Greek—*porneia, por-ni'-ah;* adultery, incest, fornication, and idolatry.

These are the definitions from the Hebrew and Greek Bibles for the meaning of adultery and fornication. They basically have the same meaning; we just translated them into English to mean two different things. If you study it, adultery in Hebrew and Greek means what we call fornication, adultery and incest. Let's now read the words of Jesus...

> And there went great multitudes with him: and he turned, and said unto them, If any man come to me, and hate not his father, and mother, and wife, and children, and brethren, and sisters, yea, and his own life also, he cannot be my disciple. *And whosoever doth not bear his cross, and come after me, cannot be my disciple.*
>
> Luke 14:25–27 (KJV)

Wow! Powerful verses! Jesus said to be a true disciple of Him you must follow Him no matter what the cost! Listen to me, I have led plenty of people to Christ and watched them fall away because of their mother, brother, or friend's opinion of what they were doing for Christ. Let me ask you this question: are you willing to miss God's best for your life because of someone else's opinion? No matter who they are? If the disciples, like Paul and Peter, were not willing to die for Christ (and they did) you might not be reading this now. If our forefathers, who came to America so they could freely follow Christ and obey God's Word, were not willing to die (and many did) for that freedom, would you be here today? Search your heart; how committed to Christ are you? Are you willing to stay out of sin and walk in purity? Are you willing to wait for God's best concerning His sending you a mate? Please know that all sin stems from selfishness and having to have everything you want when you want it and not considering the ramifications your actions, or lack thereof, have on others. Please search your heart and find out where you really stand.

And he went through the cities and villages, teaching, and journeying toward Jerusalem. Then said one unto him, Lord, are there few that be saved? And he said unto them, Strive to enter in at the strait gate: for many, I say unto you, will seek to enter in, and shall not be able. When once the master of the house is risen up, and hath shut to the door, and ye begin to stand without, and to knock at the door, saying, Lord, Lord, open unto us; and he shall answer and say unto you, I know you not whence ye are: Then shall ye begin to say, We have eaten and drunk in thy presence, and thou hast taught in our streets. But he shall say, I tell you, I know you not whence ye are; depart from me, all ye workers of iniquity. There shall be weeping and gnashing of teeth, when ye shall see Abraham, and Isaac, and Jacob, and all the prophets, in the kingdom of God, and you yourselves thrust out. And they shall come from the east, and from the west, and from the north, and from the south, and shall sit down in the kingdom of God. And, behold, there are last which shall be first, and there are first which shall be last.

Luke 13:22–30 (KJV)

Did you read that? Jesus said it was a narrow door to salvation. That's right, not everyone goes to heaven! Jesus said that workers of iniquity had to depart from His presence. Are you a worker of iniquity? Will you enter into the straight gate? It is a wonderful blessing to have peace and joy, knowing you are in God's will for your life. If you are having sex before marriage, you are not in God's will for your life. Look what Timothy says:

Now in a large house there are not only gold and silver vessels, but also vessels of wood and of earthenware, and some to honor and some to dishonor. *Therefore, if anyone cleanses himself from these things, he will be a vessel for honor, sanctified, useful to the Master, prepared for every good work.* Now flee from

76

youthful lusts and pursue righteousness, faith, love and peace, with those who call on the Lord from a pure heart.

2 Timothy 2:20–22 (NASB)

Lay hands suddenly on no man, *neither be partaker of other men's sins: keep thyself pure.*

1 Timothy 5:22 (KJV)

Are you a vessel of honor or dishonor? Are you keeping yourself pure? Is disobeying God's Word worth the consequences? Before you pray for a mate (or anything else for that matter!) you need to obey this scripture below which tells you not to let sin reign in your body and to present the members of your body as instruments of righteousness to God:

Therefore do not let sin reign in your mortal body, that you should obey it in its lusts. And do not present your members as instruments of unrighteousness to sin, but present yourselves to God as being alive from the dead, and your members as instruments of righteousness to God. For sin shall not have dominion over you, for you are not under law but under grace.

Romans 6:12–14 (NKJV)

No matter what you have done, you can be forgiven. The word *repent* means to turn from sin and turn to God. Confessing your sin to God is step one, but the next step is actually turning away from sin. I have had Christians tell me they were married to someone in their heart so they were not in sexual sin. This is about the dumbest thing I have ever heard, and I have almost always heard this from women. One, it is unbiblical. Two, if someone won't stand up publicly with you in front of a minister, family, and friends and say wedding vows with you, what are you doing with them? Do you believe their lame excuses, or are you making excuses for them? Love is giving, not taking. Love will give their life to you and will stand at an altar with you. True love will find a way. If it is finances, then have a smaller wedding! There is no real excuse for disobedience to the Word of God.

Every person is to be in subjection to the governing authorities for there is no authority except from God, and those which exist are established by God. Therefore whoever resists authority has opposed the ordinance of God; and they who have opposed will receive condemnation upon themselves. For rulers are not a cause of fear for good behavior, but for evil. Do you want to have no fear of authority? Do what is good and you will have praise from the same; for it is a minister of God to you for good. But if you do what is evil, be afraid; for it does not bear the sword for nothing; for it is a minister of God, an avenger who brings wrath on the one who practices evil. *Therefore it is*

necessary to be in subjection, not only because of wrath,
but also for conscience' sake.

Romans 13:1–5 (NASB)

This passage is referring to the civil government. Paul tells you in Romans to obey your government. Of course, if your government tried to force you to sin or renounce Christ, the higher law is obedience to God. However, our government has specific laws in which a union between a man and a woman is considered a marriage. Obeying these laws is not a sin and is the biblically correct way to go. When I got married (in Texas) the law was that we had to go to court to obtain a marriage license and say our wedding vows in front of someone who was licensed or ordained by law to perform a wedding ceremony. Legally and in the eyes of God, we were not married till we fulfilled our government's law for marriage. More importantly, marriage is a covenant, like God has a covenant with us. A covenant is a written or verbal agreement where there is a sacrifice. When you are truly married in God's eyes, you will have at least a verbal commitment with someone where you are leaving behind (sacrificing) your single life, leaving your parents to start a new home, and becoming one with your new spouse.

He that loveth his wife loveth himself. For no man ever yet hated his own flesh; but nourisheth and cherisheth it, *even as the Lord the church: For we are members of his body, of his flesh, and of his bones. For this cause shall a man leave his father and mother, and shall be joined unto his wife, and they two shall be one flesh.* This is a great mystery: but I speak concerning Christ and the church. Nevertheless let every one of you in particular so love his wife even as himself; and the wife see that she reverence her husband.

Ephesians 5:28b-33 (KJV)

At the marriage altar, you are leaving your old life behind and starting a new one. It is a covenant commitment, like our God made a covenant with you, with His son being the sacrifice. No matter what the movies or the media promote, what God says in His Word is what should be held above everything else in your life.

And the multitude sat about him, and they said unto him, Behold, thy mother and thy brethren without seek for thee. And he answered them, saying, Who is my mother, or my brethren? And he looked round about on them which sat about him, and said, Behold my mother and my brethren! For whosoever shall do the will of God, the same is my brother, and my sister, and mother.

Mark 3:32–35 (KJV)

Jesus is very clear in Mark 3, when His mother, Mary, came to see Him. He said that His brother, sister, and mother were those who did the will of God. He fully indicated that if His mother did not do God's will, she would not qualify as His mother. If Jesus said that about Mary and His natural-born brothers, what does He say about you? Are you in God's will for your life? Do you want to be? First, you must repent of all sin. That means confess your sin to the Lord and then turn completely from all sin. Please read the next two scriptures out loud.

> If we confess our sins, He is faithful and just to forgive us our sins and to cleanse us from all unrighteousness.
>
> 1 John 1:9 (NKJV)

> I acknowledged my sin to You, and my iniquity I did not hide. I said, I will confess my transgressions to the Lord [continually unfolding the past till all is told]—then You [instantly] forgave me the guilt and iniquity of my sin. Selah [pause, and calmly think of that]! For this [forgiveness] let everyone who is godly pray—pray to You in a time when You may be found; surely when the great waters [of trial] overflow, they shall not reach [the spirit in] him.
>
> Psalm 32:5–6 (TAB)

If you have been in sexual sin, and want to start over with a clean slate before the Lord, please pray this prayer out loud and with a sincere heart. Remember, to be forgiven you must forgive others! (Mark 11:25–26)

Dear Lord,

I have been in sexual sin and I am sorry, please forgive me. I am asking You right now for an extra measure of Your grace and power to walk in holiness and purity before You. I choose to turn from sin now, and offer the members of my body to You as instruments of righteousness. I also forgive anyone who has ever mistreated me. In Your Son Jesus' name, amen.

Let not sin therefore reign in your mortal body, that ye should obey it in the lusts thereof. Neither yield ye your members as instruments of unrighteousness unto sin: but yield yourselves unto God, as those that are alive from the dead, and your members as instruments of righteousness unto God. For sin shall not have dominion over you: for ye are not under the law, but under grace.

Romans 6:12–14 (KJV)

CHARLIE'S STORY

(NAMES HAVE BEEN CHANGED)

Have you ever wondered if God works through your friends?

This is something I had never put much thought into until I met a truly Christian couple that lived all aspects of their lives for Christ.

I met Luke and Bethany at one of our apartment complex's social events, and we quickly became friends. Both Bethany and Luke encouraged me with their testimony of how the Lord brought them together; Bethany suggested I write down all the qualities I was looking for in my future wife. When I finished, I had a two-page list! We prayed for my mate and about a year later, she showed up! The person God intended for me to spend the rest of my life with was right in front of me at church. I was an active member of our church's young adult group. Heather* was also attending the group and when we made eye contact and I saw the gleam in her eye, my heart would beat quickly. We spoke to each other at events, and during the weekend of our fall church retreat, I received a revelation in my heart that she was the one God intended for me to spend the rest of my life with. At one of Bethany's Bible study meetings, Bethany prayed for me, and the Lord showed her a picture of Heather at church with me. I had not told Bethany I was interested in anyone, and I had never told her about Heather. When Bethany told me what the Lord had showed her, I grinned like a Cheshire cat. Bethany then gave me a word from the Lord: "Talk to her about it" (marriage). A few days later, I took Heather to dinner and told her I really believed we had a future together and that I wanted to pursue a deeper relationship with her. She told me it was about time I realized it! After that night, Heather decided to put off going to China to teach. Between January and March of 2004 Heather and I developed our friendship, but it was not until the day after my birthday that we had our first date. I took her to see the movie The Passion of the Christ. From then on it was an express train in getting to know each other.

One night we headed to the mall because I needed to get some new shoes, and we ended up looking at engagement rings. I could tell she was surprised but excited at the same time. After we looked at rings, I wanted to make this occasion extra special by using some of the diamonds I had inherited from my great,

great, great grandmother. I had her engagement and wedding bands custom made. The week before I was planning on asking Heather to marry me, I met her parents and requested their permission and blessings to marry their daughter. On Heather's birthday, I picked her up for dinner and took her to my place for a four-course meal. At the end of the meal, I mentioned I had one last item to give her. I got down on one knee and told her I would be honored if she would become my wife. She instantly said yes! We got engaged at 7:38 PM. From there we went to her parents' house where they had a small party waiting for us to celebrate. We married a short time later in my home church. I thank God daily that He placed Heather in my life. God truly answers prayers! Heather is a 100 percent match to my mate list.

> So they are no longer two, but one. Therefore what God has joined together, let man not separate.
>
> Matthew 19:6 (NIV)

IS THERE REALLY A HELL?

And as it is appointed unto men once to die, but
after this the judgment.

Hebrews 9:27 (KJV)

As a Christian, it is really important that you realize
you have an enemy named Satan who wants to destroy
you and does not want you married to a godly spouse.
Whether you are single or married, he will try to deceive
you and get you to follow him knowingly, or unknow-
ingly. Since Satan loves to destroy marriages and pre-
vent Godly ones from happening, it is important that
you know how to submit to God and resist the devil.

Submit yourselves therefore to God. Resist the
devil, and he will flee from you.

James 4:7 (KJV)

The first time I ever experienced anything in the demonic realm was one night when Jessie and I were visiting her parents in Florida during Thanksgiving. When I was lying in bed, something jumped on me and started choking me. I cried out, "God! God help me!" Then I felt two beings come out of me through the soles of my feet. I had just given my life to Christ for the first time that summer and a year prior to that I didn't even believe in the Christian God, and especially not in Satan. After that happened, I told Jessie's mom, who was a Christian, and she just acted like that was a normal thing and did not make a big deal about it so I didn't either.

Another day, when I was still living in New Orleans and by myself (and sober!), God gave me a vision of hell. In the vision I was sitting at a bar with my room-mate Jessie. The bar was very dark and dreary with a stage and overturned tables and chairs all around. We were very thirsty and extremely lonely; we both kept waiting for someone to come and get us, but no one did. The only thing to drink was hard liquor with no ice or anything else to mix it with except more hard alcohol. Desperate, I walked outside the bar looking for help. I can still remember how incredibly lonely and thirsty I was. When I walked out of the bar, I saw a tall building, about twelve stories high. There were some people sitting on the steps, but they had dark sockets for eyes and very gray skin. I heard gunshots from one of the upper stories and then people screaming. I knew someone had been murdered. Then the entire building was engulfed in flames and everyone burned up.

All of a sudden, the building reappeared with the people and I watched the whole scene again. It appeared that they were chained to whatever their ruling sin was and had to experience it forever. When I came to, I realized that God had showed me where drunkards go when they die. Did that stop my drinking? Unfortunately not. There was another time when I saw a demon actually sit up out of my body; the next thing I knew, it looked like I was levitating a few inches off my bed. One of the scarier things that happened to me was when a huge demon pulled my spirit man out of my body and held me up against the wall with one hand wrapped around my neck. I remember looking down at my body lying there. When I cried out to God, the demon let me go and I went back into my body. All of these events I have told you about happened *after* I said the salvation prayer from my heart, meaning every word and had received the Holy Spirit and was water baptized. But, I was still drinking and partying. Now, after I started walking in holiness, I still sometimes have had trouble with demons jumping on me and trying to choke me, especially at night, but none have taken my spirit out of my physical body again.

Please, stay away from sin! When you sin, you are bowing your knee to Satan and giving him authority in your life. Stay away from witchcraft and all dark arts. If you have been involved in these types of activities, repent and ask God to lead you to an experienced deliverance minister. It is harmful, no matter how inno-cent it appears. And yes! Christians *can* have demons. I was at a friend's house one time and when they started praying for me (I had been walking close to the Lord by this time for a couple of years), a huge demon inside me threw me off their couch. At a Bible study one day, a group of people surrounded me and started praying for me. All of a sudden (and I was filled with the Holy Spirit) a big demon walked out of me in front of every-one. I could fill several pages with personal experiences I have had. I definitely believe in Satan, demons, and hell, but if you choose not to believe me, please believe God's Word about hell and who goes there.

> Not every one that saith unto me, Lord, Lord, shall enter into the kingdom of heaven; but he that doeth the will of my Father which is in heaven. Many will say to me in that day, Lord, Lord, have we not prophesied in thy name? and in thy name have cast out devils? and in thy name done many wonderful works? And then will I profess unto them, I never knew you: depart from me, ye that work iniquity.
>
> Matthew 7:21–23 (KJV)

Notice, in the above scriptures, that Jesus was talk-ing about Christians, people who called Him Lord, who prophesied (and it did not say false prophecy), drove out demons, and performed miracles, but they do not get to enter heaven. Why? Look at the last sentence—it was because they were in sin. That's right; you can say

Jesus is Lord, work miracles, and still go to hell if you "are a worker of iniquity." *Hell,* you say? God would never allow anyone to go to hell. Really? Do you only believe part of the Word of God? If you don't believe in the entire Word of God, you cannot really believe Jesus is your Lord because the Bible is where it says He died for your sins and rose again. Here are a few scriptures in God's Word about hell (or Hades). In the Hebrew, hell is called Sheol.

Hell (Greek)—*hades; hah'-dace Hades,* place of departed souls.

> The LORD is known by the judgment which he executeth: the wicked is snared in the work of his own hands. Higgaion. Selah. *The wicked shall be turned into hell, and all the nations that forget God.* For the needy shall not always be forgotten: the expectation of the poor shall not perish for ever.
>
> *Psalm 9:16–18 (KJV)*

Did you read that? Does that sound like a God who does not allow anyone to go to hell?

> And it came to pass, that the beggar died, and was carried by the angels into Abraham's bosom: the rich man also died, and was buried; *And in hell he lift up his eyes, being in torments, and seeth Abraham afar off, and Lazarus in his bosom.* And he cried and said, Father Abraham, have mercy on me, and send Lazarus, that he may dip the tip of

his finger in water, and cool my tongue; for I am tormented in this flame. But Abraham said, Son, remember that thou in thy lifetime receivedst thy good things, and likewise Lazarus evil things: but now he is comforted, and thou art tormented. And beside all this, *between us and you there is a great gulf fixed: so that they which would pass from hence to you cannot; neither can they pass to us, that would come from thence.*

Luke 16:22–26 (KJV)

Notice in the above scripture that Jesus said the rich man in Hades was being tormented and in agony in the flames. There is nothing in the scripture about a purgatory. The Word is very clear: when you die, it is either heaven or Hades.

And I saw a great white throne, and him that sat on it, from whose face the earth and the heaven fled away; and there was found no place for them. And I saw the dead, small and great, stand before God; and the books were opened: and another book was opened, which is the book of life: and the dead were judged out of those things which were written in the books, according to their works. And the sea gave up the dead which were in it; and death and hell delivered up the dead which were in them: and they were judged every man according to their works. *And death and hell were cast into the lake of fire. This is the second death. And whosoever was not found written in the book of life was cast into the lake of fire.*

Revelation 20:11–18 (KJV)

And the twelve gates were twelve pearls: every several gate was of one pearl: and the street of the city was pure gold, as it were transparent glass. And I saw no temple therein: for the Lord God Almighty and the Lamb are the temple of it. And the city had no need of the sun, neither of the moon, to shine in it: for the glory of God did lighten it, and the Lamb is the light thereof. And the nations of them which are saved shall walk in the light of it: and the kings of the earth do bring their glory and honour into it. And the gates of it shall not be shut at all by day: for there shall be no night there. And they shall bring the glory and honour of the nations into it. *And there shall in no wise enter into it any thing that defileth, neither whatsoever worketh abomination, or maketh a lie: but they which are written in the Lamb's book of life.*

Revelation 21:21–27 (KJV)

Okay, so now that you know there is a hell, where is it? Let's see...

Hell from beneath is excited about you, to meet you at your coming; it stirs up the dead for you, all the chief ones of the earth; it has raised up from their thrones all the kings of the nations.

Isaiah 14:9 (NKJV)

Now that he ascended, what is it but that he also descended first into the lower parts of the earth?

Ephesians 4:9 (KJV)

But if the LORD make a new thing, *and the earth open her mouth, and swallow them up, with all that appertain unto them, and they go down quick into the pit;* then ye shall understand that these men have provoked the LORD. And it came to pass, as he had made an end of speaking all these words, *that the ground clave asunder that was under them: And the earth opened her mouth, and swallowed them up,* and their houses, and all the men that appertained unto Korah, and all their goods. They, and all that appertained to them, went down alive into the pit, and the earth closed upon them: and they perished from among the congregation. And all Israel that were round about them fled at the cry of them: for they said, *Lest the earth swallow us up also.*

Numbers 16:30–34 (KJV)

For as Jonas was three days and three nights in the whale's belly; *so shall the Son of man be three days and three nights in the heart of the earth.*

Matthew 12:40 (KJV)

From these scriptures we can conclude that hell is actually in the center of the earth! If you believe the rest of God's Word about how His Son Jesus Christ died on a cross for your sins and rose again three days later to sit at God's right hand, then you must also accept that there is a place of eternal torment for people who do not receive Jesus as their Lord and Savior and repent of sin. (Remember, repent means to turn away from sin and turn to God!) If Jesus Christ really is Lord of your life, you would stay away from sin because if you are really following Him, He would lead you away from sin, not towards it. From my testimony in chapter one, you read how Satan tried to stop my marriage to Luke by using some of our loved ones. Satan also tried to ruin my life by sending me his choice of men to marry before I met Luke. I know that many Christians like to avoid Satan and downplay his role in their lives, but that does not mean he is still not out there trying to deceive them from walking in the will of God for their lives. When you are believing God for a mate, please pray and ask God to reveal to you any of Satan's deceptions in your life so that you do not get married to the wrong person! There are a couple of reasons someone who should be married isn't. Sometimes you and/or the other person are not ready yet and you need to wait for God's timing. Another reason could be that Satan is interfering with the Holy Spirit bringing you and your mate together. Sometimes this can come in the form of you believing some of Satan's lies. For example: "No one is going to want me because I am divorced with three kids" or "Nothing has ever worked out for me before, why should it now?" Some other demonic lies go like this: "All men want is sex" and "There are no good men/women out there." The only way that you can know for certain is by asking God to reveal to you what the block is to you getting married. Another book I wrote, called Born of the Spirit, teaches you how to know for sure whether or not something in your life—and this can apply to receiving a mate too—is born of God. I suggest that you read Born of the Spirit as a follow up to this book.

DINING WITH THE KING

One day at work before I was married to Luke, but after my divorce, a friend came to visit me. He wanted to pray with me about forgiveness because God had laid it on his heart that I needed to forgive men in general. So I prayed a simple prayer of forgiveness towards men with him, and when I did, it felt like a huge burden lifted off me. The scripture came to mind, "The love of God is shed abroad in our heart by the Holy Ghost" (Romans 5:5, KJV), and I suddenly felt a pure love towards men, including my ex-husband and other men who had hurt me. I had truly forgiven them. What started me having such bitterness towards men?

First, my biological dad left my mom, but while he was married to her, he ran around on her and I would watch him abuse her. When he was married to his second wife, I would occasionally visit him. During those visits, I watched him hit her, snort cocaine and smoke pot. Their marriage ended when he beat her so bad she was put in the hospital. When my mom found out, I didn't get to see him for several years; my mom was constantly mad at him because he didn't pay child support. After some time had passed, my mom thought it would be a good idea for me to go live with my biological dad and his third wife. I lived with him and his third wife and two step-daughters for two years in a suburb outside of Chicago when I was about twelve years old. I witnessed him get drunk on a daily basis and then of course take it out on his family.

As a child, I didn't have many friends. When my mom and dad divorced, I thought it was because of me, and I would take this out on other children. I was highly jealous of children who still had a dad, so I used to steal some of their things to hurt them. Now, my step-dad considered me his own, but to a confused little girl, it just wasn't enough! Please listen to me, divorce has long reaching effects on children; be careful who you marry! The Bible says that *"the wages of sin is death"* (Romans 6:23, KJV) and that doesn't just mean spiritual death either. As you can imagine, I was very unpopular all through grade school and I just became more resentful and bitter when the popular kids didn't like me. Once in a while, I would have a boyfriend, but I usually was mean to them so those relationships were always short lived.

When I got out on my own and realized that at sixteen there are not too many high-paying jobs out there when you haven't even graduated high school, I had to find a way to pay the bills. When I went to visit my biological dad, to see if he would help, he took me to a strip club and told me that those girls made around $300 a night. I was still a virgin, very inexperienced, and I wanted to leave that bar immediately. Also somewhere during that time he showed me blueprints of a gentlemen's club that was about to open in his town and told me that my grandmother was one of the investor's and he was to be one of the night managers. Appalled, I went back to Houston. A few months later, after I turned seventeen, a new girl named Tammy checked into our school; she was very beautiful and wore expensive clothes. I was easily impressed and when she had to sit next to me in English class, I went out of my way to befriend her. Soon afterwards, she confided in me that she was an entertainer at a very nice gentlemen's club in Houston. She painted a glamorous picture and encouraged me to try it. I didn't at first, but when I realized that I just could not support myself on an almost minimum wage job and attend high school, I gave in.

Tammy and I were roommates for over a year, and during that time she posed for Playboy magazine for a special edition they were doing on strip clubs. After that, men tried to date me to meet her, and the root of rejection deepened in me. Living with her was exciting, we even ran off to L.A. together to see if we could "make it." That didn't last long since we got tired of sleeping in our car parked on a street behind the Hollywood sign and eating canned refried beans (at that time a can of beans was about fifty cents!). So back to Houston we went. One night Tammy and I went and worked at the new gentleman's club my grandmother had invested in per my dad's request. However, I was tired of this lifestyle and still in high school, so when my dad asked me to move to Florida with him I did. When he failed to find work, I again had to work at a local club in town at night after school to pay the bills. The second semester of my senior year in Florida, someone found out I worked at a strip club and it got around my school. My drama teacher asked me to not attend her classes anymore, and the principal tried to kick me out of the school. By this time I was eighteen and legally allowed to be working in those clubs, so I had to stand my ground with the school and I was able to graduate. I was still fully supporting myself and my dad during that year and after all of the long nights of work and early mornings at school, I was determined to finish.

All of the men I dated that I met in this line of work cheated on me, only wanted a fling, or had abusive personalities. (I met my ex-husband at one of these clubs in New Orleans, and you already know the result of that relationship!) I tried desperately to numb my pain with drugs and alcohol. I worked at these types of clubs for approximately five years, mainly in Houston, Florida, and New Orleans. One night, when I was coming off a cocaine binge, I again almost committed suicide. It is only by the grace of God that I am alive today and you are reading this.

If you have hatred, bitterness, or resentment toward the opposite gender, it is time to forgive. I had to be healed of my unforgiveness and bitterness towards men before I married Luke or it would have caused devastating problems in our marriage. When I realized that God sent a man, not a woman, to die for my sins, it was a real eye opener. You must walk closely with the Lord and allow Him to heal you of past sufferings. Sometimes it is a step-by-step process that takes time, but He will heal you as you hold tightly to Him, pray, and obey His Word. It is very hard to have a healthy marriage when you are holding on to rejection, hatred, and bitterness. There are plenty of excellent ministries that deal with emotional healing; some that have helped me are Joyce Meyer Ministries and Paula White Ministries. One of the most remarkable emotional healings I received was from Dr. Aiko Hormann Ministries: Soul Restoration Series. After my husband and I went through that series together, I felt like a whole new person. Joyce Meyer also wrote an excellent book that I recommend: *The Root of Rejection.*

I also had a huge fear of commitment that became more prominent after my divorce, but God delivered me from that one night. He gave me a dream and in the dream He showed me how He places two people together for the purpose of marriage. God showed me a person's heart and Him dropping a seed in the heart of who the person's mate was. Then the seed was watered with friendship and it began to grow into a tree with more love and friendship (sunshine and rain) until it blossomed into marriage. He revealed to me that He puts two people together with friendship and a godly love, not lust like the world does. Lust can turn into hatred very quickly. When I woke up, the Lord spoke this very clearly to me: *"Commitment is the doorway to freedom."* Ask yourself: are you willing to forgive and let go of people who hurt you? Are you willing to allow God to heal your heart? If so, start by praying this prayer:

Father God,

I have been holding unforgiveness, hatred, resentment, and bitterness toward others and especially toward (men/women). I forgive all (men/women) who have hurt me, and I ask that You now forgive all of my sins and wash them away with the blood of Jesus Christ. Jesus said He came to bind up the brokenhearted, so please bind up my broken heart and set me completely free of all unforgiveness, hatred, resentment, and bitterness. I accept Your forgiveness and healing now, in Jesus' name, amen.

RACHEL'S STORY

(NAME'S HAVE BEEN CHANGED)

I first dedicated my life to Christ when I was fifteen but decided that obeying the Bible was a little overrated and partying with my friends was more fun. I was the type of person who constantly had to have a boyfriend; I had to have attention. Guess what? I ended up pregnant, unwed, and still in high school. My baby Julie* was born two weeks after I graduated. Even though I had made mistakes, I desired a daddy for Julie. I knew I had to get my life straight and if I did, God would give me the desires of my heart. I rededicated my life to Christ at twenty and started learning His Word. Christine, who was working with my mom at the time, told her about how she witnessed the Lord put Luke and Bethany together. I decided to meet with Bethany, and she shared her testimony. We prayed for God to send my mate, and I wrote a three-page list of characteristics

I wanted in a husband. In less than a year, I met Scott*
at church.

At first, we were just acquaintances, and I didn't
think twice about him romantically. After all my pain
concerning romantic relationships, I had asked the Lord
to seal my heart and protect it till He sent His choice to
me. Also, I finally learned to be content being single. I
was friends with his sister, and when I invited her to my
birthday party, she asked if she could bring her brother
Scott with her. I said okay and didn't think anything
of it. While he was at my birthday party, he invited me
to his birthday party, which was the next day. While I
was busy putting on makeup in the dining room during his party, Scott was in the kitchen cooking, and we
just started talking. We hit it off immediately, and I saw
something in him I had never seen before. We talked
through most of the night, and I invited him to my
dad's church the next day, which was Father's Day. We
started dating in June, and Scott proposed in Novem-
ber. It was the most romantic night of my life; we went
to an Italian restaurant with some friends, then on a
horse and buggy ride through downtown Houston. He
took me back to Transco Tower where the waterfalls
were, dropped to one knee, and asked me to be his
wife. I knew in my heart of hearts he was the one God
had for me, and he was a 100 percent match to my
mate list.

At our wedding ceremony, after Scott gave me my
ring, he gave Julie her own ring and promised to be her
daddy and take care of her. God is very faithful, and I

am grateful for His grace and mercy in my life. Here is a sample of some of the things I wrote on my mate list:

Good looking, a cutie; blond hair, blue eyes, at least 6 feet tall (Scott is 6'2"), clean cut with good hygiene.

Godly leader, committed to the Lord on a daily basis, not a fake, someone who would be a spiritual leader in our house and would be my friend and a confidant.

Has a desire to work with young people.

Someone who was practicing abstinence, was okay if had previously made a mistake, but was saving himself for marriage now.

A pure love, no lust involved, trustworthy, someone who respects me enough not to make a move till our wedding night.

Someone who accepts me for who I am and will forgive me for my past and who would be willing and ready to be a daddy for Julie.

Someone who would treat me like a lady and encourage me emotionally, mentally, and spiritually.

Someone who would get along with my family and who my family would love.

Someone different from the type of guys I had met or dated before.

Today, Scott and I have a brand new baby boy, and I give the glory to God for giving me the family I always desired.

LET'S PRAY FOR THAT MATE!

When asking the Lord to send you a mate, first and foremost, they have to be a Christian.

> *Do not be unequally yoked together with unbelievers.*
> For what fellowship has righteousness with lawless-
> ness? And what communion has light with dark-
> ness? And what accord has Christ with Belial? Or
> what part has a believer with an unbeliever? And
> what agreement has the temple of God with idols?
> For you are the temple of the living God.
>
> 2 Corinthians 6:14–16 (NKJV)

How do you know for sure if someone qualifies as a believer? Read these scriptures.

> Little children, *let no man deceive you: he that doeth*

righteousness is righteous, even as he is righteous. He that committeth sin is of the devil; for the devil sinneth from the beginning. For this purpose the Son of God was manifested, that he might destroy the works of the devil. *Whosoever is born of God doth not commit sin;* for his seed remaineth in him: and he cannot sin, because he is born of God. In this the children of God are manifest, and the children of the devil: whosoever doeth not righteousness is not of God, neither he that loveth not his brother.

1 John 3:7–10 (KJV)

In case you are still unsure how to tell if someone is really a Christian, read this:

But among you there must not be even a hint of sexual immorality, or of any kind of impurity, or of greed, because these are improper for God's holy people. Nor should there be obscenity, foolish talk or coarse joking, which are out of place, but rather thanksgiving. For of this you can be sure: No immoral, impure or greedy person—such a man is an idolater—has any inheritance in the kingdom of Christ and of God. Let no one deceive you with empty words, for because of such things God's wrath comes on those who are disobedient. Therefore do not be partners with them. For you were once darkness, but now you are light in the Lord. Live as children of light.

Ephesians 5:3–8 (TAB)

Please read those scriptures carefully! My ex-husband and I were in sexual immorality along with plenty of impurity. The above scriptures clearly explain that such people (and notice this scripture is from a letter written to the Christians at Ephesus, *not* to unbelievers) will not have any part in the kingdom of God and that we are not to be partners with people, even "Christians," who partake in immoral behavior. When you do not know the Word of God (or do know it and choose to disobey) it is easy to be deceived and think someone has been sent from God to marry you. Rule number one for singles waiting for a mate is: *"If God sends you someone, they will be following Jesus!"*

I have prayed with many people and watched God send a mate. I have always noticed that when the Lord sends a mate, the mate draws them closer to the Lord, not further away and certainly not into sin. Remember my long list that I wrote containing everything I wanted God to send me in a husband? Luke is a 100 percent match. When I pray with singles, I always have them write down on paper what the desires of their hearts are concerning a mate. Without fail, the Lord has always sent them a 100 percent match. Why a list? Because when you pray for something, you need to be specific. I also believe God puts the desires of His heart in your heart—even the desires for the qualities in a mate you are looking for.

In the Old Testament, the Holy Spirit did not live inside of us, and our hearts were "wicked and deceitful" (Jer. 17:9) and you could not trust them. Now, in the New Testament era when you are born again, God takes out your old stony heart and gives you a new heart of flesh (Ez. 36:26). Also, it says that God, Jesus, and the Holy Spirit will make their home inside you (John 14:23). You cannot always trust your *emotions,* but if you are born again and walking holy before the Lord, you can trust your heart! Remember, the love of God has been shed abroad in your heart by the Holy Spirit (Rom. 5:5) and as long as your motive is love, God's love, your faith to pray for a mate will work. The Bible says faith works by love (Gal. 5:6). Also, the Bible says that singleness is a gift from God (1 Cor. 7:6–7). If the thought of being single for the rest of your life is horrifying, you have obviously not received the gift of singleness. The Lord Jesus will always give you the grace and favor to do what He has purposed in His heart for you.

The first few items I wrote on my mate list were what I wanted my husband to look like. That might not sound very spiritual and may be even a little selfish, but if you are not physically attracted to someone and you marry, it could be devastating to the other person who has to live in a marriage with a spouse who does not find them attractive. Would you want to marry someone who does not find you attractive and desirable? Of course not, so it is wise to marry someone you are physically compatible with. God will not give you a snake when you have asked for a fish (Matthew 7:7–11). Also, please do not list a quality for your mate out of fear. When I first did my list, I was afraid God was going to send back my ex-husband and make me marry him (a couple of other Christians told me this, and I naively believed them!) so the first thing on my original list was that my new husband would be over six feet tall. I figured since my ex was only about 5'10" this would give me a loophole, and I wouldn't have to get back together with him. Remember, I was a young Christian who believed just about everything any Christian told me. Knowing what I know now, I know the Lord does not send His daughters abusive men to marry, and my ex certainly had not changed! When God revealed to me I wrote that on my list out of fear, I removed it.

While you are making your list, make sure what you write down is out of love and faith. Check your motives! Before I pray with a single for their mate, I go over the purity scriptures and get ample assurance from them that they are going to wait till their wedding night, no matter what they had done in the past.

How do you pray for your mate? I prayed every way I knew; I did not stop storming heaven for a mate until I was engaged! I must admit, I prayed many times out of fear because I was afraid God wouldn't send me anyone, and I would be single for the rest of my life. Early in my Christian walk, another Christian told me I could not get remarried because I had been through a divorce. The Lord revealed a scripture to me that quickly dispelled those fears.

For the unbelieving husband is sanctified by the wife, and the unbelieving wife is sanctified by the husband: else were your children unclean; but now are they holy. But if the unbelieving depart, let him depart. A brother or a sister is not under bondage in such cases: but God hath called us to peace.

1 Corinthians 7:14–15 (KJV)

My unbelieving ex-husband filed for a divorce and left; I did not want the marriage dissolved and was willing to work it out. He was not. According to the above scripture, I was not bound in such circumstances. Also, in Matthew 19:8–9 (KJV):

He saith unto them, Moses because of the hardness of your hearts suffered you to put away your wives: but from the beginning it was not so. And I say unto you, Whosoever shall put away his wife, except it be for fornication, and shall marry another, committeth adultery: and whoso marrieth her which is put away doth commit adultery.

If your spouse commits fornication (sex outside of wedlock), you are permitted to divorce, but you do not have to. I used to cry alone in my apartment because I thought God could not find anyone to love me. Looking back, I see that neither Luke nor I were ready for marriage, and if the Lord had brought us together any sooner, one of us, if not both, would have probably messed everything up. Hindsight is always 20/20, and if I had not been so fearful and insecure, I could have enjoyed my singleness more. I cannot brag and say that

I prayed and just left meeting my mate in God's hands like I should have. Instead I shed many tears of loneliness and drove my friends crazy by insisting that they pray with me (a lot!) for the Lord to send my mate. There is a point you should get to in your Christian walk, where God leads your prayer life and lets you know when and what to pray for instead of you trying to lead or boss God around. I was in the bossing-God-around stage. But God is patient and merciful and still answered my prayers! To truly have your heart's desires line up with God's, you *must* spend time with Him in prayer (maybe even fasting!) and reading His Word. To birth out God's promise in your life, including a mate, you must be intimate with Him on a daily basis! Please, before you make your mate list, pray, surrender your will to His, and ask Him to place His desires for your life in your heart.

Did you do that? Good. Next step, read the following scriptures out loud (including saying "It is written" before the scriptures, because that is how Jesus spoke to the devil! (see Matthew 4). By repeating these scriptures out loud, it increases your faith to pray for your mate. Do that several times and even for a few days if necessary to get them deep in your spirit. Do not miss any of these steps as they are equally important.

It is written: *with God all things are possible (Matt. 19:26, KJV).*

It is written: *Verily, verily, I say unto you, He that believeth on me, the works that I do shall he do also; and* *greater works than these shall he do; because I go unto my Father. And whatsoever ye shall ask in my name, that will I do, that the Father may be glorified in the Son. If ye shall ask any thing in my name, I will do it (John 14:12–14, KJV).*

It is written: *Verily, verily, I say unto you, Whatsoever ye shall ask the Father in my name, he will give it you. Hitherto have ye asked nothing in my name: ask, and ye shall receive, that your joy may be full (John 16:23–24, KJV).*

It is written: *And Jesus answering saith unto them, Have faith in God. For verily I say unto you, That whosoever shall say unto this mountain, Be thou removed, and be thou cast into the sea; and shall not doubt in his heart, but shall believe that those things which he saith shall come to pass; he shall have whatsoever he saith. Therefore I say unto you, What things soever ye desire, when ye pray, believe that ye receive them, and ye shall have them (Mark 11:22–24, KJV).*

It is written: *faith without works is dead (James 2:20, KJV).*

As you can see from these scriptures, you must ask the Father in the name of His Son Jesus Christ. The first thing on your list when asking for a mate is that they are a Christian who obeys the Word of God and stays out of sin. The Bible is very clear that you should not be unequally yoked with unbelievers. Ephesians 5:5–7 states that you should not be partners with people who practice sin. One last thing before you pray: check your heart motives and make sure you are praying out of love. The Bible says that faith works by love, so for your faith to produce the desired results, your motive needs to be love (Gal. 5:6). Did you surrender your will to the Lord? Did you ask Him to place His desires for your life in your heart? Did you read the above scriptures several times each out loud? Are you ready to pray for a mate?

Here is the prayer. First, write in the blanks everything you desire in a mate and then pray the prayer out loud. You must *believe* in your heart that it is done already in the spirit realm after you pray.

Father God,

I come boldly before Your throne with thanksgiving in the name of Your Son Jesus Christ.

Thank You for everything You have done for me. Thank You for my country, all the leaders in my country and all the leaders in the body of Christ. Thank You for having mercy upon us all (1 Timothy 2:1–4). Father God, You said in Your Word that anything I asked of You in the name of Your Son Jesus Christ, that You would do it. I ask You now in Jesus' name to send me a Christian mate who obeys You and has all of these following characteristics:

BETHANY K. SCANLON

I believe You are sending this person into my life, and I ask that when they come, that You will reveal to both of us by your Holy Spirit that it is Your will for us to marry. I also ask for a special gift of discernment, so I know right away when someone is not the right person. Thank You for answering this prayer, I now ask that the "peace of God that surpasses all understanding would keep my heart and mind through Christ Jesus" (Philippians 4:6–7). Amen!

Now that you have prayed, it is done. When is God going to send your mate? I do not know; it could be tomorrow, it could be years. You have to take that up with Him. Also, He may lead you occasionally to pray more for a mate, or to pray for your mate. Sometimes, we have to intercede, pray in tongues, and birth out God's promise for our life. The Bible states that what is born of God will overcome the world (1 John 5:4). That means you, your mate, and your marriage need to be born of God and obey God if you expect a long, happy marriage that will overcome tough situations. I have seen many long marriages, but the only joyful, peaceful ones I have seen are the ones where both people truly put God first and not just attend church or call themselves Christians.

Now that you have prayed, what do you do? Easy. Go to church and get involved in the singles group or Bible studies, etc. There are also Christian on-line dating services for single Christians who are at least eighteen years of age. Be open to going on dates assuming you are "of age" and ready for marriage. Do not be double minded; if someone does not match your list, do not date them.

If you have to go on a date or two to see if they are a match, fine, but do not get involved if they don't. The Bible says that a double-minded man shouldn't expect to receive anything from the Lord (James 1:6–8). If you pray for someone who matches your list, and then turn around and date someone who is opposite of what you prayed for, then you are double minded. If you want to meet a Christian mate, you need to be where the Christians are. It is perfectly okay to meet a mate in a singles class in your church. I have heard some say that going to church to meet a mate is wrong. If you are one of those people, ask yourself—where do you expect God to send you a mate? Why would it be okay to look for a mate in a smoke-filled bar with a bunch of drunken people but not in His house among His people? (Plus, you should already have a home church or church body that you are associated with.)

Do you expect someone to just knock on your door or walk up to you at work and say, "Hi! God told me to marry you!"? What would you do if that happened? If some man had knocked on my door or showed up at work and had done that, I would have run for the hills. I have heard things like that happening, and am sure for some it does, I do not doubt that, but typically it does not. Also, I hear very few stories of people hearing an audible voice from God telling them someone is their mate. Even though it did happen for me, I was not looking for it and it might not happen to you, so please be open to how God wants to bring someone into your life. Learn to be led by your spirit man and *always* let peace be the final umpire and judge in all matters, not voices. If I ultimately did not have God's inner peace in marrying Luke, I would not have done it. The Bible says in 1 Corinthians 14:33 (KJV), "*For God is not the author of confusion, but of peace, as in all churches of the saints.*" If you think someone is your mate and there is a lot of confusion and no peace, walk away. Place the situation in the Lord's hands and pray till you get your peace back. Wait and see what the Lord does. Since God says that faith without works is dead, get out there!

FINAL THOUGHTS...

I think that a lot of people miss what God wants to do in their lives because of ideas in their heads about how God is going to bring His will about through them. It is important that you pray and ask God to reveal to you His plan and timing for you to receive your mate.

You also must be what you want to attract. If you are trying to attract a godly mate who is led by the Spirit of God, you need to be a godly person who is led by the Spirit of God. Women, if you want a man to love and respect you for whom you are, don't try to attract him with your looks and your body. Dress appropriately and modestly. I am not saying to be unfashionable and not look good, but don't dress specifically to attract a man with your body.

Men! Watch your eyes! Jesus said in Matthew 5:27–29 (KJV):

> Ye have heard that it was said by them of old time, Thou shalt not commit adultery: But I say unto you, That whosoever looketh on a woman to lust after her hath committed adultery with her already in his heart. And if thy right eye offend thee, pluck it out, and cast it from thee: for it is profitable for thee that one of thy members should perish, and not that thy whole body should be cast into hell.

I have always found it disgusting when I would talk to a man and he would look me up and down. If you want women to respect you, you need to show them respect.

> No man can serve two masters: for either he will hate the one, and love the other; or else he will hold to the one, and despise the other. Ye cannot serve God and mammon
>
> Matthew 6:24, (KJV)

If you date and marry someone for their money and not their relationship with Christ, you are not truly putting God first. Women, if you force a man to jump through hoops to catch you, he just might make you jump through hoops to keep him. I have seen women demand that men take them to fancy restaurants and buy expensive gifts. I also have seen women put guilt trips on a man if he doesn't call every night or play by her unspoken rules. Do you want him to demand that you stay a size two your whole life, even after three kids, and never get wrinkles? The Bible says God is not mocked, that whatever a man sows, so shall he reap. Lighten up and treat the other person like a friend, not a servant!

Men! Don't chase money but get a good career! You are to represent Christ in your marriage, and He is the best provider there is.

> But if anyone does not provide for his own, and especially for those of his household, he has denied the faith and is worse than an unbeliever.
>
> 1 Timothy 5:8 (NASB)

> This should be your ambition: to live a quiet life, minding your own business and working with your hands, just as we commanded you before. As a result, people who are not Christians will respect the way you live, and you will not need to depend on others to meet your financial needs.
>
> 1 Thess. 4:11–12 (NLT)

Follow Christ and He will provide you with a career or business that earns enough income to support a family! To both men and women, stay away from sexual sin; use common sense! Do not let yourself be in a position or place where you are tempted.

Here is a list of questions you need to ask yourself when you do meet someone:

Do they put God first in action and not just words?

Do they do the things they say they are going to do? Do their actions line up with their words?

How do they treat singles of the opposite gender whom they would not consider dating? This is especially true for men who are visually stimulated. How does he treat women whom he thinks are ugly?

Watch what they laugh at. Do they laugh at things they shouldn't find funny?

Do they walk in holiness and refuse to be involved with you sexually until after the wedding?

Do they only attend church to impress you?

Who are their close friends? I am not talking about the people they minister to; I am talking about their close friends with whom they share themselves. Do they avoid deep relationships with godly friends or are they afraid of accountability?

Have they been faithfully staying out of harmful behavior (sexual sin, excessive amounts of alcohol, drugs, stealing, lying, witchcraft such as horoscopes, Ouija boards, etc.), or do they only go for a season and then fall back into old and destructive habits?

Do they passionately pursue what they believe the Lord has called them to do?

Do they pursue money, fame, or success or do they seek after the Lord? How do they handle finances?

Most importantly, be led by the Holy Spirit in your decision for a mate. If you are unsure how to be led by the Holy Spirit, two fantastic books that explain it (I urge you to read them both!) are *How to be led by the Spirit of God* by Kenneth E. Hagin and *How to Hear from God* by Joyce Meyer.

So what about marriage? How do you put God's kingdom first concerning your marriage? The Bible has plenty to say on marriage; Luke and I wrote our marriage vows according to the following scriptures:

And further, you will submit to one another out of reverence for Christ. You wives will submit to your husbands as you do to the Lord. For a husband is the head of his wife as Christ is the head of his body, the church; he gave his life to be her Savior. As the church submits to Christ, so you wives must submit to your husbands in everything. And you husbands must love your wives with the same love Christ showed the church. He gave up his life for her to make her holy and clean, washed by baptism and God's word. He did this to present her to himself as a glorious church without a spot or wrinkle or any other blemish. Instead, she will be holy and without fault. In the same way, husbands ought to love their wives as they love their own bodies. For a man is actually loving himself when he loves his wife. No one hates his own body but lovingly cares for it, just as Christ cares for his body, which is the church. And we are his body. As the Scriptures say, "A man leaves his father and mother and is joined to his wife, and the two are united into one." This is a great mystery, but it is an illustration of the way Christ and the church are one. So again I say, each man must love his wife as he loves himself, and the wife must respect her husband.

Ephesians 5:22–33 (NLT)

The husband must fulfill his duty to his wife, and likewise also the wife to her husband. The wife does not have authority over her own body, but the husband does; and likewise also the husband does not have authority over his own body, but the wife does. Stop depriving one another, except by agreement for a time, so that you may devote yourselves to prayer, and come together again so that Satan will not tempt you because of your lack of self-control.

1 Corinthians 7:3–5 (NASB)

If you are truly seeking God's kingdom first, these scriptures will be acted out continually when you are married. Obeying God's Word and praying together will safeguard your marriage. If you choose not to marry someone who is obeying God's Word, you are in for a world of hurt and you will not be living God's best for your life. You alone cannot carry a marriage; it has to be both of you working together, committed to obeying His Word. I was praying for one of my girlfriends about why the Lord had not sent her mate yet, and He told me, "If I sent her husband right now, she would rebel against his authority." Does this mean you are to be a doormat? No! Husbands are also supposed to submit to their wives in love and love them like Christ loves the church. The whole point is to keep both of you and your house in harmony. If your mate does not know how to walk with God and obey Him, you are going to go through a lot of unnecessary trouble in your marriage. May God bless you and send you your mate!

SALVATION

If you do not know Christ, and would like to, please read along as I go over God's Word concerning salvation:

> If we confess our sins, He is faithful and just to forgive us our sins and to cleanse us from all unrighteousness.
>
> 1 John 1:9 (NKJV)

> I acknowledged my sin to You, and my iniquity I did not hide. I said, I will confess my transgressions to the Lord [continually unfolding the past till all is told]—then You [instantly] forgave me the guilt and iniquity of my sin. Selah [pause, and calmly think of that]! For this [forgiveness] let everyone

who is godly pray—pray to You in a time when You may be found; surely when the great waters [of trial] overflow, they shall not reach [the spirit in] him.

Psalm 32:5–6 (TAB)

The Bible states that you should confess your transgressions (sins) to God and He will forgive you. Jesus also said that you must be born again to go into God's kingdom:

There was a man of the Pharisees, named Nicodemus, a ruler of the Jews: The same came to Jesus by night, and said unto him, Rabbi, we know that thou art a teacher come from God: for no man can do these miracles that thou doest, except God be with him. Jesus answered and said unto him, *Verily, verily, I say unto thee, Except a man be born again,* he cannot see the kingdom of God. Nicodemus saith unto him, How can a man be born when he is old? can he enter the second time into his mother's womb, and be born? Jesus answered, Verily, verily, I say unto thee, Except a man be born of water and of the Spirit, he cannot enter into the kingdom of God. That which is born of the flesh is flesh; and that which is born of the Spirit is spirit. Marvel not that I said unto thee, *Ye must be born again.* The wind bloweth where it listeth, and thou hearest the sound thereof, but canst not tell whence it cometh,

and whither it goeth: so is every one that is born of
the Spirit.

John 3:1–8 (KJV)

Paul writes in Romans that you must believe in your
heart and confess with your mouth that God raised
Jesus from the dead and that Jesus is your Lord.

That if thou shalt confess with thy mouth the
Lord Jesus, and shalt believe in thine heart that
God hath raised him from the dead, thou shalt
be saved. For with the heart man believeth unto
righteousness; and with the mouth confession is
made unto salvation.

Romans 10:9–10 (KJV)

Are you ready to receive salvation? Are you ready to
completely turn from your sin and serve the Lord Jesus
Christ? Do you know that serving Him isn't always a
bed of roses and that you may still have rough times
but you will now have God's Holy Spirit helping you
through them? As long as you are well aware of what
you are doing, here is the prayer to be forgiven of your
sins and be born again. (You must pray this out loud
and believe in your heart. Remember, Romans said to
confess with your mouth and believe in your heart.)

Almighty God,
I come before You humbly and with thanksgiving. I
know that I have sinned against You and I am asking for
Your forgiveness right now. I am truly sorry and I ask You

for an extra measure of grace to serve You and to stay away from sin. I chose to forgive other people who have hurt me, and I thank You for forgiving me. Please guard and protect me all the days of my life and help keep me from evil. I commit my life to You and Your Son Jesus Christ right now. I believe in my heart that Your Son Jesus Christ who walked on this earth in the flesh, died for my sins on a cross and then rose from the dead three days later. This Jesus is now my personal Lord and Savior. I ask You, Father God, to please fill me now with Your Holy Spirit. I am now born-again. In Jesus' name, amen.

What now? Now you must cultivate a relationship with the Lord by spending time with Him and reading His Word. The book of John says that "God is the Word and the Word is God." Pray every day. Ask the Lord to lead you and guide you to the church He has for you. When looking for a home church, look for the following.

Do they say that Jesus Christ is Lord of all and the only way to heaven?

Do they encourage you to read and study His Word?

Do they teach holiness and warn you to stay away from sin?

Here is a daily prayer you can pray to get you started in your relationship with the Lord.

Father God,

Thank You, Lord, for Your goodness and mercy! Thank You for _____! I completely surrender my will to Yours. I come boldly before Your throne of grace right now (Hebrews 4:16) in the name of Your Son Jesus Christ. Please place your full and complete armor on me now (Eph. 6:10). I ask Your Holy Spirit to please bring order to my day today and to the rest of my life. Lord, [this is where you talk to Him; you can ask Him questions, ask Him to meet any needs you have—whether physical, financial, emotional, etc.— pray for leaders, friends, parents; forgive anyone you need to; repent of any sins you have committed, etc.]

Amen!

OTHER BOOKS BY BETHANY K. SCANLON

Born of the Spirit
Ever wonder why some things in your life just don't work out? This book reveals how to know whether or not something is born of God in your life. Have you ever doubted God's ability to work things out the way they are supposed to? Then this book is for you!

Redeeming Catholics and Their Catholicism
(co-authored with Christine Dickson)

This is the story of one Catholic's journey to know God through the help of a friend. Christine and Bethany give real life accounts of answered prayers and miracles that they have seen in their lives. This book also gives sound teachings according to God's Word and can be used as a Bible study and journal.

Where's my money?
Have you been frustrated and discouraged because you have not seen the promises of God manifested in your life concerning your finances? Are you wondering where your open heaven of blessings is? Bethany tells her story of how God walked her through the Bible, teaching her about His will concerning her finances.

New Life
Have you ever wondered how to use the Word of God for different situations in your life? This book/Bible study shows the reader how to apply God's Word to their life to break free from strongholds like and anger, fear, and condemnation.

Searching for Liberty, Grace and Destiny
This four part fiction novel takes you on an adventure with three different women, Liberty, Grace and Destiny. See through their eyes as they struggle in their life and watch as God walks them through some very trying times.